Imagine
Being

Imagine Being

IN A LIFE YOU LOVE

Kristin
Andress
&
Jaqui
Jeanes-Lowry

Imagine Being Press
www.ImagineBeing.com

Published by Imagine Being Press

Imagine Being Press
127 Reynosa Court
Solana Beach, CA 92075
858-793-0919
www.ImagineBeing.com

To order additional copies, go to www.ImagineBeing.com.

Cover and interior design by JENNINGS DESIGN
(www.jenningsdesignonline.com)

www.ImagineBeing.com web site designed by E-websmart.com
(www.e-websmart.com)

ISBN: 978-0-615-34705-9

LCCN: 2010921897

Printed in the United States of America.

10 9 8 7 6 5 4 3 2 1

Kristin
*To you who endeavor to use
your imagination to dream about all that is possible in life . . .
and then have the courage and vigor to live it!*

Jaqui
In loving memory of my parents, Jean and Charles Henry.

The authors of Imagine Being in a Life You Love *are from the United States and United Kingdom. Where applicable, British spellings have been maintained.*

CONTENTS

ACKNOWLEDGMENTS

*T*here are many special people who have helped us on our journey to create this book. We have tried to acknowledge you here, though sometimes words cannot completely describe the deep gratefulness in our hearts.

Kristin Andress

I acknowledge my mom for being the light in my life and my steadfast supporter through the missteps and the significant changes. You are the one that made me believe anything is possible and taught me through the tough times, to get on with it, and in the good times, share and celebrate them. You inspire me.

I acknowledge my dad for loving me so much and being my biggest fan. You cheer me on, help me to know how to laugh and have fun, and make me realize that no matter what, you will be there. And, Rita, for your continuous encouragement, I thank you.

I acknowledge my stepdad, Russ, for accepting me in every way and making our lives joyful while you were here.

I acknowledge my brothers, Scott and Kent, who I love, often miss, and always respect. You are my big brothers and my protectors.

I acknowledge my extended family, each one of you, for allowing me to be part of your lives and for influencing my path. We have experienced years of life together, and I feel blessed because of it.

I acknowledge my friends, the true gifts in my life. I will not name you here for fear I may omit someone, but you know who you are, and I will be reminding you of what you mean to me. Truly, I could not ask for better friends. Your belief in me astounds me. I love you so much.

I acknowledge C.O. for bringing me to my knees in prayer each night and for being a light in my life when times were dim. You are my star, alongside Sarge.

I acknowledge Jaqui for taking a stand for me when I had no true idea what that meant. She saw in me something I could not see for myself and allowed me no excuses in working toward my transformation. You are a wizard in the best of ways, and I am amazed and awed by your spirit, your talent, and your giving. Thank you, dear coach, friend, and now . . . co-author.

I acknowledge Stedman for being an example of enjoying what he does to his core and for the many discussions regarding the world happenings and what we can do to help.

I acknowledge God. Thank you for giving me a voice.

Jaqui Jeanes-Lowry

I acknowledge my husband Nick for his amazing tolerance while I worked on the book early mornings, late into the evenings, and over the weekends. Thank you for being so patient with me when I got stuck on some of the work. You helped me focus, and your attention to detail was very helpful.

I acknowledge Michelle Graham who works with me in the VSA business. Thank you for all your listening, reviewing, and research for the book. Thank you for the contribution you have been in my life and the inspiration you are for others.

I acknowledge VSA New York—Angelo, Tony, and the team—for their mentoring, guidance, and coaching over the past decade. Your coaching is masterful.

I acknowledge Landmark Education for its coaching over the years and the contribution Werner Erhard has been in my life. He inspires me to be the best person I can be. I acknowledge Dr. Deepak Chopra for his teachings and his fabulous courses.

I acknowledge my many mentors and friends who have made a difference to me, including Murray Reid, Geoff Hill, Andrew Harvey, Louise Durose, and Amanda Phillips. Special thanks to all my clients, who allowed me to contribute to them and who have contributed to me since. A big thank you to all of my friends, who encourage me through the setbacks and keep me true to the life that I imagine for myself.

Thank you, Kristin, for inviting me to be your co-author on this magnificent journey. You are a dear friend and an inspiration to the women of the world.

From Both of Us

Thank you to Judy Emmert for helping to make our dream come true with your editing, your listening, and your partnership. You are truly gifted.

Thank you to all our friends who gave their stories so that they may help many others in the world, too: Amanda, Andy, Betty, Candace, Mrs. Dunn, Becky, and Michelle. You are very generous, and we appreciate the time and energy you gave. To Sukeena and Miriam for their stories for the future work we do.

Thank you to the reviewers who have been patient in reading through the material—Sue, Michelle, Louise, Tony, Angelo, and Ken. Your feedback was precious.

Thank you to Erica Jennings for the design work and to Michelle Tjemeland for designing our web site.

Thank you to all of you who wish to participate in creating your life so that you love living it each day, and for giving us many reasons to serve as best we can in the world.

PREFACE

*L*ike many people, New Year's Eve is a special time for me—a nostalgic day that allows me to reflect on what has transpired during the year ending . . . an enchanted evening that rouses my spirit in anticipation of the year coming.

It is both an ending and a beginning, an opportunity to acknowledge the chances that have passed me by, and to set a new course that will bring me closer to the life I truly desire.

And so it was that on one particular December 31, I sat outside my new home in sunny San Diego reminiscing about the past twelve months and writing my intentions for the new year. It was a simple exercise in clarity and focus, an examination of what I had accomplished and what I still needed—and would choose—to do.

What I had accomplished three months earlier was realizing a dream that had been seven years in the making. I had moved to California, a place that had long appealed to my sense of freedom and liberation. The sunshine, the Pacific, the interesting collection of people—many of whom were transplants like myself—seemed to fill the state with an energy that I wanted to experience. After spending my entire life in Illinois and Missouri, I was ready for the challenge of moving across the country. I knew I would grow from the move and, ultimately, find my true path in the world.

When asked why I relocated to an area where I knew so few people, I typically respond that I want to "box myself in, so I can box myself out." San Diego is a melting pot for personal development, a wellspring of inspiration. I am surrounded by the likes of Tony Robbins, John Assaraf, Ken Blanchard, John Maxwell, Jack Canfield, Deepak Chopra, Debbie and Arielle Ford, and Brian Tracy. For someone who has long believed in the power of personal development, my new home represents the ideal place to begin realizing the life I want.

So there I sat that December afternoon, pleased that I had found the courage to make the move. And while I fought off the subtle pangs of loneliness that sometimes accompany new surroundings, I suddenly began to feel something else totally unexpected—uncertainty. It quietly crept upon me as I sat there, building in intensity until it finally grabbed me tightly in its grasp. The truth was, underneath the bravado of taking on a new, unfamiliar world, I was not clear on what I specifically intended to be or do as a result of living in this new geography—or with my life in general. And . . . I'd just reached age forty. Despite the decision to cause change for myself, I felt I was still standing still in my life, not moving anywhere close to where I wanted to be in my personal and professional relationships.

As I thought of my intentions for the coming year, I realized I had no idea of where to begin. I called upon that inner voice to console me: "Wait! I'm the person who, when it comes to personal development books and seminars, has been there, done that. I've got the T-shirts to prove it." As convincing as that voice tried to be, I still struggled to write my plan for the coming year.

Until it suddenly dawned on me . . . I don't need to create the entire plan for my life on simply this symbolic New Year's Eve day. I only need to begin. I realized that the coming year—and every year to come after it—needed a process much simpler and more fun than the life-changing grand plan I found myself trying to write—and then figuring out how to achieve (aka—overwhelm!). If I wanted the life and lifestyle I always imagined having, I had to begin by ignoring the surroundings of my ideal world and access the *ideal* me.

Simply put, I had to check in with Kristin and ask her: Do you know what is available to you? Do you know how to get what you want? Do you realize how your thoughts change your life and how your actions will change it further? Do you know what happy is? Do you know you are the cause? Are you aware of the contribution you must be to the world? Are you ready to get on with it? And most importantly, are you willing to help others who might spend their New Year's Eves—or any selected day of defining personal intentions—struggling with the same uncertainty?

That is how this book came to be. What I learned about myself that day—and what I subsequently found to help me imagine and secure the life I truly desired—was the impetus for this book. And I chose to pass it on to those of you reading now, who, I imagine, are looking for a bit of guidance and insight, too.

As I made the decision to bring *Imagine Being* to life, I frankly could not imagine doing so without my trusted and supportive listener, coach, and confidante as part of this journey. Jaqui Jeanes-Lowry changed my life a few years ago. Through her coaching, I experienced transformation, and the continuation of her gift is that this possibility is now threading its way to so many others. I asked her to be my co-author, my partner in this journey for you. (Thank you, Jaqui.)

Imagine Being is a powerful tool to help you establish and fulfill your intentions, your dreams, and your possibilities—in essence, to create a life you love. It is a guide for learning who you are, defining and creating the purposeful life you imagine living, and managing the setbacks that arise in the process of achieving and sustaining your dreams. It helps you navigate through the thoughts, behaviors, and actions inherent to realizing the life you love, and holds you accountable for choosing to create your life by design rather than by chance. It inspires you to be a light and contribution in the lives of others. In short, it can change your perception of what is possible in your lifetime.

We hope this book will help you envision the life you want, access that core being who is not hesitant to go after what you truly desire, realize you are the cause of your life's desires, and imagine being the person you long to be.

Kristin Andress
January 2010

✦INTRODUCTION:
IMAGINE BEING IN A LIFE YOU LOVE

So, our first question to you is this: **How is life going for you?** Is it going in the direction you imagined it would? Are you living the life you always wanted? Are the dreams you set in motion still spinning, or have they stopped and left you feeling incomplete? Have you reached the point where you are taking inventory of your life?

This is what we know about what happens in the process of living: When we are not in the presence of it, we are not present to it. As humans, we often put off designing the lives we love until it is too late. We tend to believe that we have all the time in the world—although our time here is finite. The time to begin authoring the design of your life is now. Don't put off until tomorrow what you must be considering today, whether it is attention to your children, health, marriage, finances, spirituality, or other need. Your time has come to actively participate in your own life.

Imagine Being is about stepping into the intention of living your life *with* purpose and *on* purpose. It's about seizing the very core of your being to participate in the present moment . . . every minute, every hour, every day.

We live in a world where we are defined by what others see on the outside. The happy family. The good job (if we still have one). The nice home. The luxuries that at one time seemed important to us. But what's on the outside is not always the true picture of what lies beneath—what's really on the inside. What's in the core of our being. It's that core that truly defines us.

Health experts tell us that our true strength comes from having a strong core in our body. It's that muscular middle section that allows us to stand tall and provides us with a healthy internal system.

Spiritualists tell us that the central core of our being is where we will find that place of divinity within ourselves. It's that contented soul that allows us, as humans, to find heaven here on earth.

However, the most important truth is what life tells us: That to achieve what we truly desire, we have to look inside at the core of our being and engage its spectacular dreams, its infinite possibilities, and its boundless energy.

Maybe you are one of those who desire to begin something new, to fill what's been missing in your life, or to scratch the itch of "I sense I need to change." Maybe you know that what you are being and doing sloughs off to ripple in a concentric circle to those around you, and those around them, and so on and so on. You know that how you show up in the world affects you and others. Maybe you know you are not quite doing or being what you had always imagined.

Our second question is: What will make you happy?

What role will you play in your own life that will make you content with it? If you had access to the "how to," would you use it?

This book is about how to live a life you love. It is possible to do, and we will show you how.

We'll focus on strengthening the core of your being by helping you recognize those areas within you that give you the power to realize your dreams.

- You, being the *cause* of designing your life

- You, being the *opportunity* maker in your life

- You, being the *reason* for momentum in your life

- You, being the *energy* responsible for your life

- You, being the *light* that guides the way for others

You are, after all, the creator of your catalysts . . . as well as your chaos. You would do well right now to realize that without a strong core, you are not in control of your life.

Our third question is this: Are you ready to imagine being?

What have you imagined being? Have you realized any of those dreams? What do you imagine being at this point in your life?

It could be that you feel you have lost your ability to imagine. It could be that your imagination is vibrant, and you merely need a bit of a push to the "what's next."

Remember this: The stuff of life will always get in the way of achieving the life we love, especially if we are not consciously considering who we are and realizing that we cause the happenings of our life. However, it is never too late to imagine being. Never.

If you want to be an active participant in your life—to become the person that you have always wanted to be—then consider those you love (including yourself) and declare your initial intention:

I will participate in my own life.

_____

(Sign here)

_____

(Date)

Kristin's Story

Growing up, I had a lot of angst. I was a smart and intuitive kid, but I was always chubby. I imagined being little, like some of my parents' friends' daughters.

My parents divorced when I was six years old, and I imagined being in a family that had two parents at home. My brothers were cool and fun, and I imagined being one of them. When I was not outside or with friends, I was daydreaming and making up stories.

I imagined being a writer, and I imagined being on a ranch in Texas, where a gorgeous cowboy loved me and we rode horses all day. I filled up dozens of spiral notebooks with stories from my imagination—including the places and people I wanted to see and be—and they swept me off to dreamland. To this day, I keep paper with me wherever I go, and definitely on my nightstand in case an idea or a character appears.

I often imagined being someone I was not. I imagined being Olivia Newton-John in *Grease*, singing, dancing, and being skinny enough to wear those leather pants. I imagined being Scott Baio's or John Travolta's girlfriend. I imagined being Brooke Shields in *Blue Lagoon*.

As a girl, I imagined being rich. We had all the money that we needed, but too often I saw my mom work two and three jobs and come home so tired. I heard my dad worry. It seemed that money was the solution to the fears and the insecurity and the worry. Always the worry.

As a teenager, I revolted a bit. I was one of the "wild" kids, partying and staying out late. I knew what some of my friends' parents were saying about me, and felt badly that they could not see beyond that wild streak to realize that I was often the one who looked out for their kids or kept them safe. I imagined being understood by them.

I grew up in a small town, where I was most often preoccupied with the dream of being anywhere but there. I imagined being the prettiest and the most popular girl in school, the one my high school crush was interested in. I dated a bad boy who was older than me and imagined being his wife. I never was. I did end up marrying a wonderful person, but what I had envisioned a wife to be was not what I became. While I don't imagine being a wife anymore, I do imagine being in love. I imagine being in a "paired" life with a wonderful guy, rather than single.

In my early twenties, my brother Kent died, and I imagined being able to remove the pain for my other brother, my parents, and myself. In my late twenties, my stepdad died, and I imagined being the person to remove the misery for my mom.

I was in an abusive relationship a year after my marriage, and I imagined being found out. I imagined being judged. Sometimes what you fear happening is exactly what should happen. I imagined being safe and in harmony, and so I left to create a new environment for me and my beloved dog.

In many ways, I should have failed at life. The cards were stacked a bit against me. But I prevailed. I received my education through scholarships, the help of grandmothers, and through loans and jobs. I imagined being strong, courageous, and tenacious. I imagined being much more than okay. I imagined being the best at who I am. I imagined being in front of my naysayers, with fame and fortune, and having a moment of sweet vengeance—although I don't care about that anymore.

Now, I just imagine being "me." I finally like me. And when someone tries to take that away through improper treatment or pushing me to do or be what I am not, I simply resist—and I persist at being me.

Today, I still imagine being thin, but I focus more on being healthy—injury- and pain-free—and fit mentally, physically, and emotionally.

I imagine being famous—only if it is because of something I've done that matters, that has impacted lives and the trajectory of our futures.

I imagine being rich, because struggle is unsettling, and wealth allows you to do amazing things for others.

I imagine being stress-free.

Being in love.

Being secure.

Being pain-free.

Being worry-free.

Being sabotage-free.

I imagine being able to make the right choices all the time, and realizing that the choices I do make are in the right time.

I imagine being a person who does not miss anyone . . . but I imagine I always will.

I imagine being the recipient of an Oscar for Best Screenplay and thanking Mom and Dad, and my dog, C.O. (I also imagine being in the seat next to George Clooney.)

Mostly, though, I imagine being in a world where we love more than we hate, and where we can work and perform and feel peace concurrently.

I imagine being baggage-free, with the bad choices I've made in my life placed curbside and remaining there as I drive away to the next destination.

I imagine being an intentional present.

I imagine being peaceful and happy, and doing purposeful work that I love, with people I love. I imagine love in my life and a beautiful, happy home. I imagine being the person that people turn to for help and guidance.

I imagine being a right-hand person to Bono, doing the work of the ONE Campaign, serving and communicating the "good" stories of people creating miracles on less than a dollar a day. Of people contributing their voice, their time, their money because they imagine being part of the collective community and they know that their humanity is also that of their brother or sister in the street.

I imagine being in a world where we do not mind taking care of one another.

I imagine being the scribe that enables and empowers each of you to create the lives you've always dreamed of living.

I do not have children, so I imagine being a mother in the larger sense, a woman who nurtures and protects children, animals, and people. I imagine taking my place on the center stage, standing up for human and animal rights, being the voice for the possible and the reflection of the collective heart.

I imagine being at the gates of Heaven one day and hearing God say, "It took you a while, but well done." I imagine being a humble, grateful servant.

I imagine being.

Jaqui's Story

As a little girl, I loved to dream. I loved to imagine what my life would be and where it would take me. Growing up in Leeds during the '60s and '70s, and as a teenager spending a lot of time in London, I was inspired by the musicians and athletes who had captured the imagination of so many young people. Dreaming was easy—and free—and so I filled my days thinking of all that I could be.

I imagined being a singer. I would entertain the other kids in the school playground and pretend I was on *Top of the Pops*, a popular TV programme. I would sing the songs of the bands Mud and Slade. In fact, I went to see Mud at the Town Hall when I was twelve years old, and it was one of the most engaging, vibrating, energy-charged days of my life! Just being at the Town Hall was as daunting as it was exciting; it is an enormous, historic building—a palace in sheer size—opened by Queen Victoria in 1858. It reflects wealth, power, and confidence, and is used as a courthouse and concert hall, and for royal celebrations. The sheer opulence and magnitude of the building left me breathless.

I imagined being a dancer. I would dance to Tiger Feet and the strains of "Jailhouse Rock." I am forever grateful to my friend who showed me how to harness my inner rhythm. From this dear friend, I learned passion and timing—and even a bit of the Twist, which was never my favorite dance. When I was older, I took ballroom dance lessons and happily grooved through the "Gay Gordon," Cha, Cha, Cha, and the Tango. To this day, I love to dance!

I imagined being a world-class gymnast, just like Russian sensation Olga Korbut. She was amazing to me because of her size—all that sheer power packed into that tiny body. She showed me that physiological limitations do not have to stop you from realizing your dreams. I worked very hard in gymnastics, but, unfortunately, my skills only enabled me to reach school-level competitions.

I also imagined being the top 200-metre athlete in the world. I remember standing many times on the podium at the Olympics and receiving my gold medal. Alas, in the real world, I only got as far as placing fourth in the Leeds City finals as a teenager.

My more realistic dreams brought me closer to earth than the rarefied circles of entertainers and Olympic athletes. For a long time, I imagined being a shoe shop assistant. Even though my mum would say that I could be whatever I wanted to be when I grew up—such as a nurse or doctor or lawyer or teacher—I always responded with "I would like to be a shoe shop assistant." Why? The truth was, I simply loved shoes.

During those early years, I also remember imagining myself to be a doctor, but not a medical doctor. I did want to heal people, but I was not thinking of helping bodies to heal. I was more interested in people's minds and what made them behave the way they did . . . sometimes funny, sometimes cruel.

What I never imagined back then was that the path I would follow later in life would be a direct result of my mum's health issues. When I was fifteen years old, she had a nervous breakdown. I clearly remember the day. We were heading home from the supermarket suddenly my mum threw the two shopping bags down onto the ground. I immediately focused on the potatoes rolling down the hill and ran to collect them. When I turned around, my mum was sobbing. She kept repeating that she just could not go on anymore. I had no idea what had caused her to be so unhappy, but I began to blame myself for asking for too many things that we could not afford—new clothes, tickets to go places, and money for this and that. I really believed I had caused her to fall apart. I believe this experience, and other experiences of childhood, made me very interested in psychology.

As I moved into my teens and twenties, my love for music continued to inspire dreams, including being a rock star, a punk rocker, a jazz pianist, and a journalist for the NME, the music press. These fantasies did, in reality, allow me to rub shoulders with some of rock's biggest stars.

I danced with David Bowie one evening. I stood at the bar with Human League after a gig they did in Leeds. I got close to Simple Minds. I patted David Byrne, the lead singer of the Talking Heads, on the head. I met Boy George before his first big gig. I also found myself visiting one of the top A&R men for BMG Entertainment, just hanging out at his office looking at the photos of the pop stars they were promoting—TLC, Whitney Houston, and Puff Daddy—and feeling like I, myself, was a megastar.

However, during these years my dreams of helping others continued as well. I imagined "saving the world" from disasters like hunger and poverty. I imagined healing South Africa and taking a stand against apartheid.

I imagined being a university teacher and helping teenagers find their true happiness in life.

During this time, I came to realize that the great part of imagining your life was that while the exact dream might not come true, you can get close to what your heart truly desires.

I once imagined travelling the world: To date, I have been to, and fallen in love with, so many places around the globe—Hong Kong, South Africa, New York, San Diego, and most of Europe.

I once imagined running my own company and employing people: I am doing that now.

And I once imagined marrying a millionaire. The man I did marry is not a millionaire, although he is worth several millions to me in his abundant love and affection.

Today, I still have that little girl inside of me, the one who likes to dream. I imagine being an author who makes a difference in the lives of people I may never even meet, one who continues to write and inspire others.

I imagine being one of the top coaches in the world, helping world leaders, corporate leaders, and celebrities rebalance their lives so they can be inspired to use their status to bring about miracles in the world . . . such as a cure for cancer, an end to hunger and poverty, and new hope for children who are dying.

I imagine one day sitting on the sofa with Oprah, discussing the amazing changes in the world due to some intervention I have created.

I imagine living in Mallorca for six months of the year and enjoying the Spanish culture and the climate. I imagine speaking fluent Spanish—and I am committed to learn!

I imagine being mortgage-free and giving more money to people who have less so they can make ends meet. I imagine serving communities to make their worlds become what they need them to be.

I imagine being healthier than I have ever been. I imagine tackling my lifelong weight problems—and winning!

I imagine helping both my great nephews fulfill their dreams, and making a significant difference in the life of the new baby in our extended family. I realise when he is twenty-one that I will be seventy years old, but I will watch his every birthday very closely as a gauge to the next era of my own life.

As for the future, I imagine jumping and jiving in the garden with my VSA colleagues when I am in my seventies. I imagine giggling right through my eighties. I imagine playing in the sand and running in the sea in my nineties.

And most importantly, through it all, I will continue to imagine being.

Our Intention

We shared our stories because we are very much like each of you—human, with faults and flaws, sometimes stuck in hamster wheels, often doubting what's next, recovering and getting on with it. Our stories are not necessarily unique and different, but we do not mind displaying them if, in doing so, someone else benefits. We chose to write this book together because we care to impact people, even if only one life. We have different experiences from one another, but have access to similar ways to address, deal with, and overcome whatever it is that "pings" us in life. We want to be a contribution to you . . . and the world.

It is our intention to show you that it does not matter where you were born in the world when it comes to imagine being. It does not matter whether the wind that whips your face sweeps down from the North Sea or across the Sahara Desert . . . whether the land beneath you is the rocky terrain of the Andes or the rice fields of Asia . . . whether the sky above you peeks out from the canopy of a rain forest or a mountainside of Douglas fir.

It does not matter if you are Caucasian, Hispanic, African, Asian, Arabic, or Slavic. It does not matter if you are male or female, young or old, rich or poor.

Where you come from and what you are does not matter and does not inhibit you from becoming what you can ultimately be. You have the ability to be a person with a purpose-driven life. Sometimes, all you need is a little help to *imagine being*.

Core Concepts

On the following pages, we will help you get in touch with the core of your being and show you how to harness the power of imagination to start creating the life you truly desire. We will familiarize you with:

- **Lifelines**—Identifying and inviting those people who you would like to help you with the intentions for your life.

- **Box In/Box Out**—Ensuring that you put yourself in the position of having to accomplish your intentions by getting leverage on yourself.

- **PINGs**—Realizing that "stuff" will happen in life and that you must adapt, move on, and utilize what you learn to empower yourself and others.

- **The Change Equation**—Developing a system for handling sudden changes and acknowledging that you are the constant amid the change.

- **Super Champions**—Seeking those people you do not personally know who can support you with specific intentions.

- **Passive Hostility**—Recognizing the behavior that arises when you want something you are not getting.

- **LIP Service**—Changing the original definition of lip service from talk only to expanding the associated possibilities and acting on them—Living In Possibility.

- **Choice Cards**—Acknowledging that you have infinite choices available to you, as well as their results and consequences.

- **SPDs**—Accepting that you need "Special Person Days"—those days wherein you reserve the right to wallow in your "stuff" for a bit, and then recover and celebrate.

Throughout the following pages and in the workbook in the Appendix, we offer questions and exercises that will assist you in defining your goals and creating a plan for your life. Be sure to take the necessary time to answer the questions and complete the exercises, as they will allow you to truly define where you are in life as of this moment and help you to imagine where you can be.

Core Actions

Consider this story.

A young woman named Joanne Murray had quite a vivid imagination, one well-suited for her chosen line of work. She not only envisioned a successful career for herself as a writer, but also the impact her words could possibly have on the world—in particular, children. So, she imagined being . . . and took action.

Jo, as she is called by her friends, worked hard at her craft, day after day, in cafés and on trains, writing away until her book was finally completed. She went on to achieve phenomenal success, becoming a bestselling author and, subsequently, influencing the world on social, political, and spiritual levels. She did what you will need to do in order to create the life you love: *imagine being* and *take action*.

Now doing so will not guarantee that you will become a billionaire like Jo, better known to the world as J.K. Rowling. But imagine just one change in your world, one action you can take that can impact the life you desire and have a ripple effect on others around you.

Imagine being. Imagination is the most powerful tool we have for creating our intentions for a life lived *with* purpose and *on* purpose.

- It allows us to form mental images of what's missing in our lives—those things not previously experienced or yet realized.

- It provides us with the creative ability to confront and deal with problems—the resourcefulness to face any situation and chart new directions for the future.

- It inspires us—it's the fire that allows us to believe in the seemingly impossible and the energy that propels us through the doubts.

- It expands our worldview—it enables us to see into others' lives and lend a helping hand and heart.

Taking action. Whether you've imagined being a successful businessperson, athlete, or parent, this book will show you how to let your imagination run wild . . . and then harness it to become very clear on your intentions for your present and future. You'll learn how to:

- Gain control of your life by defining who you are and where you want to be
- Accept that you will have challenges and develop a belief system that will sustain your dreams—and hold you accountable to them
- Take advantage of the opportunities in life and overcome the setbacks and excuses that can hold you back
- Write a clear plan for your life through declaring your intentions and identifying the choices you have
- Harness momentum and personal power to achieve goals, and develop a lifeline to keep you moving in the right direction
- Share your gifts with others

You have begun the journey to imagine being in a life you love. Just imagine what you will discover.

PART ONE:

IMAGINE BEING THE CAUSE

Only one who devotes himself to a
cause with his whole strength and
soul can be a true master. For this reason
mastery demands all of a person.
Albert Einstein

Chance is a word void
of sense; nothing can exist
without a cause.
Voltaire

In this section, you will learn to:

- Take control of your life
- Recognize that what you cause has effect
- Take responsibility for your happiness and contentment
- Leave behind the TEMP excuses
- Define where you are and where you want to be
- Create a lifeline
- Hold yourself accountable

CHAPTER 1:

OUR CAUSE

*A*t one point in creating the concept for this book, we considered calling this section "Being the Change." However, we realized that "Being the Cause" was much more appropriate. Many people feel that life just happens to them, and it will unless *you* cause the events, the situations, the opportunities, and the miraculous you wish to manifest in your life.

We have to remember that we do cause the not-so-great stuff, too. Our choices impact the direction of our lives. That's why it is critical that we take responsibility for our choices. Even in the worst of times, when we want to blame a boss or bank or government, we must acknowledge that we played a role in it, large or small. Owning responsibility for who you are and how you turn up in the world is a giant leap toward realizing that you are the cause of being where and what you are.

This sounds simple enough, though there is evidence indicating that thousands, perhaps millions, of people do not take this responsibility. Whatever your beliefs about the welfare system or the health of other nations, you'll find quite a lot of blaming and wiping of \ hands—a lot of people saying "not mine." The reason for not taking responsibility is simple: it can be, and mostly is, difficult. Taking the right road, or the high road, is sometimes the path less traveled. Besides, it is easier to put off on someone else what you know you created for yourself (and possibly others).

In the end, however, you are 100 percent responsible for your life.

Kristin's Story

There was a time in my life when I think if I had not caused change, I would no longer be here today.

I was working constantly, in a very destructive relationship, physically exhausted and unhealthy. I was disconnected from the people who cared for me and in a state of denial to all. During a very short time, I got married, divorced, lost my brother and stepfather, was abused in a relationship, and, though I'm sounding like a country song, lost one of my dogs to liver failure. A person can let tragedies stop her, or she can let them empower her. I had a few eye-openers as to how short life is.

I was in such a spin. Even thinking of it today takes my breath away. Somehow, I knew I needed a break in the horrible routine. I was out of the destructive relationship . . . and I was really tired of my job that no longer felt like a career. The pressure and the expectations were overwhelming, and I was sinking. I didn't like myself at all.

So, I took my dog, C.O., and I rented a little cabin on Lake Michigan. For four days, I was holed away with a computer (no e-mail or Internet), my dog, and my thoughts. I took a journal, too. One day, as I sat on the beach with the wind blowing hard and the waves just rolling in, I saw an object on the crest of a wave. It would disappear and then return, again and again. As it approached shore, I recognized it as a giant beach ball, full of color and just fighting each wave as it came closer to land. I likened my life at the time to that beach ball—spinning out and going backward, then climbing the wave and toppling down the other side, then repeating, repeating. The beach ball did finally hit land, and when it did, it flew off into the distance as if certain of the direction all along. Forever, this will be my analogy for taking control of my life.

That weekend at that cabin, I wrote most of my first book. I gave myself until Thanksgiving to make a decision about going to another firm or finding something else to "do" altogether. The choice—the decision to leave the company I had been with for ten years—was already made. My fears about money and pride and whether my dad or mom or friends would still value me if I left my job were pushed aside. I was frightened to leave and even more frightened to stay.

This time, my choices were about me and what I had to give. I was learning to value myself for who I was. If that meant I had to live in a tent, I'd find the humility, forget the pride, and be happy. I read two books that put my feet solidly on the ground and my head exactly where it should be to make the most of my life: *Man's Search for Meaning* by Victor Frankl, a holocaust survivor, and, *Living, Loving and Learning* by Leo Buscaglia. These books demonstrate that, truly, anything is possible, that the heart carries us so much further than the head, that we have so much more right now in the moment than we ever appreciate, and that dealing with money issues can be as simple as having faith, exercising good judgment, and prioritizing happiness factors above it.

I took two full years off work until I was almost flat broke. I wrote and spent time with C.O. and myself. Those two years of reflection? That was the best decision I've ever made. To hell with the money I wasn't making. There are fewer times when I feel like that spinning beach ball, but I never take my eye off the goal. Times still get tough and I worry. I wonder if I'll be alone forever. I think about taking a "proper" job rather than serving as an entrepreneur. I try to stay disciplined as I learn and write and improve. I fail and I succeed. But, I make better choices and I'm happier. In the end, I follow through on my goal of living a life created and crafted by me and inspired by good people and God.

Every time I open my Bible, it flips to Chapter 1 in Jeremiah where verse 9 reads, "I am giving you the words you must speak." I so often feel this sentence is speaking directly to me, and that I ignored this message for some time due to lack of belief and confidence in myself. It has taken me a while to believe that I can truly impact the lives of others through my ability to communicate and give voice to what is possible in life. I can now imagine manifesting my destiny with the words I am given. I trust life's little coincidences. I trust myself.

Yeah, I get scared and I wonder if my investment in learning a new trade, a new industry, and moving to a new city and state will pay off . . . and then I catch myself. Because, you see, it has already paid. Through discovering what I imagine being and tuning in to my true purpose and passion, I have "me" back, a person I kinda like. And I'm close to my family, an unparalleled foundation from which to cultivate the possible. Now I don't often want for much, because I already have so much I've wanted.

Jaqui's Story

I left the world of being an employee to run my own business. I received help from the local business advisors funded by the government to help new business owners with their start-ups. I went through this process for several weeks by attending evening classes to learn about such things as tax, legal matters, personnel procedures, and where else to look for funding and resources This was all very new to my husband and me. We did not know many people who had their own business, and we had few contacts that could give advice. I had an agreement with my husband that if I did not at least cover my salary in the first six months of the start-up, then I would find a job. I was still very scared of being self-employed and making it work, even though I thought of it as being in a great adventure. I kept saying to myself, "I will make it work." It did work out. I managed to create my salary in a few months and then, within a short time, I was employing my niece and others to help me, too.

I found that being self-employed allowed me to work when I wanted to work in the type of work I was doing, which was mostly training and coaching people. I had flexibility in the hours that I worked. I could work full-out for several days at a time and then take four days off if needed. I could work better with my own energy. I do my best work when I am feeling in good shape. I continued to work in my own business for four successful years and then later asked VSA Consulting in New York if I could set up VSA in the UK with the flexibility of running my own business while being connected to the team in the States. I came about meeting VSA by taking up a course in New York that had me fly in on a Thursday and leave every Sunday for a period of thirteen weeks. People noticed me doing this crazy thing. I booked very cheap flights and hunted for cheap hotels, too.

I am lucky in my relationship with my husband that he is so supportive of everything I choose to do. We met when we were both twenty-one years old; all these years later, we still love one another and are as committed to one another as we were then. Being in a relationship for this long certainly has its challenges and we, like other couples, have found it requires both the love and the commitment to keep it going. There have been times when we could have called it a day. We have had our share of the struggle and the arguments, though we have managed to get through them. Keeping together takes mostly two things—the love for one another and the commitment to one another. The type of love changes over time—from being in love to being with a person so long that you have a deep love and regard for the other person. We also have so many memories we can share of our journey that binds the two of us together.

My health is like that of most people. There are things to handle month-to-month and year-to-year. I am asthmatic, I have an under active thyroid, and I have reached middle age. Now I need to take special care of myself and treat my body with more respect than I may have done in earlier years. The body requires attention, and it needs nourishing accordingly. I give more time to it, focus on it more, and listen to what it is telling me to do. I eat better, sleep well, relax a little, slow down as needed, boogie now and again, walk more, and drink less alcohol and more water. I fall off my intentions and then I get back on again.

It took many years (almost a lifetime) for me to wake up to how I was completely asleep at the wheel and out of control of what "I" really wanted and needed.

I was thirty-seven when I realised that what was really important to me was not luxury this and that and not to be the best at work, outperforming everyone else. Not a bigger this and much more of that.

I realised I was running out of steam. I was working far too hard and giving far too much. I hit rock bottom. It was then that I realised that I wanted to take back control of my life.

I must admit that it was a frightening time for me. I was very confused. I came to understand that while I enjoyed the essence of what I did, I did not enjoy the time invested, or even the reward received.

As I looked across from where I was to where I thought I wanted to be, all I could see was the deep and relentless bottom of the gap between here and there. I had very little idea of how to cross the valley without being gravely injured. I needed help. I needed to find people to talk to.

It became clear that the main areas of importance for me were to be healthy, to enjoy being loved, to feel financially stable, to enjoy the work that I did, and to have time for myself (and others outside of work). For me, it was about feeling a sense of freedom, feeling that I was contributing to others while being contributed to. I did not need luxury; I just wanted a lifestyle that made me happy and made my husband happy, too.

Today, at age forty-eight, I have more money than I could ever have imagined. I have a life partner of twenty-six years. I have a job I love. I am in better shape physically than I have been in fifteen years. This did not all come to me easily. I had to go through the valley again and again—and I expect I will go through many more in the future to get to where I want to be in life. Each time I go through the valley, however, I believe that life will be far better on the other side.

Summary

If you want to be the cause of your life, start by getting away to sort out your thoughts. The quiet is very loud. Don't allow distractions. Find a beach or a cave or whatever it takes, but sit down and think, and be open to whatever it is you receive. Take the first step in living life on your terms. Once you dip your toe in the river, you can't help but dive in and swim.

Whether your intention is to take stock of your life, improve your life, or take back your life, you are the cause of what you create within it. It is true that your good decisions and not-so-good decisions have a ripple effect that will impact your world. Still, we encourage you to choose and act—to *cause* what it is that you wish to manifest for yourself and for others.

CHAPTER 2:

ASSESS AND ACCESS THE LIFE YOU IMAGINE

This life is yours. Take the power to choose what you want to do and do it well.

—Susan Polis Schutz

It is your life.
And, sometimes, it just seems out of control and you want someone to blame.

This past year was a perfect example of that. In 2009, the anguished cries of millions of people could be heard amid the deepening recession that wrapped itself around the globe.

In the United States, job security was suddenly gone, real estate values sank to new lows, and retirement portfolios vanished. A *USA Today* survey revealed that 60 percent of Americans believed they were facing the greatest economic crisis of their lifetimes.

In Britain, the grim economic forecast by the British Chamber of Commerce was realized in the GDP growth remaining below trend, banks bailing, and public debt mounting.

Recession? Blame the government. Housing foreclosures? Blame the banks. Astronomical medical costs? Blame the insurance companies. Unemployment? Blame big business.

It's all too easy to blame others for the crises in our lives. Yes, we are, at times, at the mercy of those in whom we place our trust. Yet, while we have the right to feel frustrated and angry for their wrongdoings and mismanagement—and outright greed—we cannot fully assign blame to them for all the bad that has manifested itself in our lives. Responsibility for our well-being must lie with each of us.

To take back your life, you must imagine *being the cause* of what takes place in it—and across your entire lifetime.

Responsibility is even rougher when you realize you did impact someone else negatively as a result of your decisions. Throughout history, across the public and private sectors, people have tried skirting their responsibilities. We see this in the CEOs who are involved in large corporate scandals, with investor scam artists, and even with teenagers who deny that drugs or gang activities were the real issues behind the collapse of their lives or the breakdown of their communities.

Here's a tip: If you are in doubt about whether to take responsibility, consider the idea of Karma. Karma can kick you in the behind. The thought of being "paid back" for not taking responsibility just may encourage you to assume your share of it.

Assess Your Life

In order to access the life you truly imagine, you must first assess your current life to determine what role you have—or have not—played in taking responsibility for it. You must:

• Realize and accept that you alone *must* be responsible for your life.

  Most of us will have eighty years in this world. During that time, there will be any number of choices and decisions for which we must be responsible. You can certainly ask someone else to choose your direction, yet, even then, you are responsible for having asked. Each day, you have an opportunity to own your life. Accepting and embracing your responsibility is the first step toward realizing the results—or consequences—of action or inaction, choice or lack thereof. This responsibility is ultimately on you.

• Become clear regarding exactly what you must be responsible for.

  The bottom line is that you are responsible for the good, the bad, and the ugly. There is as much grace in celebrating your good as there is in taking ownership of your not-so-good. Your responsibilities are founded on choice and decision. This can pertain to how you behave, what you do/don't do, who you spend time with, what you say/don't say, what you eat/don't eat, whether you work out, how you feel, and so forth. As you assess where you are in your life, identify precisely where you need to step in and be more responsible.

+ Assess who you need to communicate with about your responsibility.

Whether it is to clear up the past or to ensure you are cleared to take ownership of the future, you must come clean with proclaiming your responsibility for the many aspects of your life. Even in arguments with loved ones, you have responsibility—even if shared. With co-workers, you may disagree or agree to disagree, and the outcome of doing so rests on your shoulders. As you take ownership, it is freeing to let others know you have made this conscious choice. In doing so, you rally supporters or you institute a measure of accountability.

+ Accept and forgive yourself for previous shortcomings.

We all have them—shortcomings. They present themselves in our ability to manage our time, our tempers, and even our oversights. We too often beat ourselves up for our shortcomings, when what we could be doing is learning from our mistakes and developing our abilities. Assess where you have not quite measured up. Decide to forgive yourself, and do better next time.

+ Ensure you learn so you don't repeat the same mistakes.

Mistakes are commonplace in life. Mistakes happen every day. They can be embarrassing and they can negatively impact our confidence. However, they are necessary to help us learn and grow. We certainly don't know everything when we enter or exit this world. It is a perpetual process of creating our knowledge base that enables us to make better and better choices. Acknowledge your mistakes—how they were caused and what can be changed to avoid a recurrence. As our knowledge grows regarding what we can cause through taking ownership of our responsibilities, we also learn how we can teach others to do the same.

Access the Life You Imagine

The truth is, if you do not accept your responsibility for being the cause of the outcomes in your life, the dissonance will fester, grow, and follow you across time until you deal with it. As much as accepting responsibility for being the cause in your life can be complicated, it does feel good to realize that the possibility to "cause" rests squarely with you.

In these times, more so then ever before, it is time to take responsibility so you can access the life you imagine. It is time to be the cause for your own life *and* for the collective whole. When you do, you can be the cause of:

- Social justice
- Economic recovery
- Business development
- Community cleanup
- Education for all
- Financial abundance
- Giving back
- Happiness in yourself and others
- Love

Your life is yours, and you have the power to choose between taking responsibility for it or leaving it to others who may not know what *you* truly want in life.

What can you take responsibility for now that will allow you to be the cause in your life . . . to imagine being?

_____

_____

_____

_____

The TEMP Excuses

Now that you have begun to acknowledge what you want to change in your life and what responsibility or actions you can take in affecting those changes, let's take a few minutes to talk about four common excuses people give for why they cannot change their lives—that is, not take responsibility. We call these the TEMP Excuses, and they stand for:

Time

Energy

Money

People

TIME—I don't have **time** to go to the gym or make nutritious lunches because I have a full schedule. I don't have **time** to write that book I always wanted to write as I work long hours. I don't have **time**

to review my finances or seek out those people who can help me with them as I don't have the **time** to research them. I don't have **time** to go out on dates as I am just too busy and too tired.

ENERGY—I don't have the **energy** to do things with my friends. I don't have the **energy** to go to the gym. I don't have the **energy** to play with the kids. I don't have the **energy** to start that new project. I don't have the **energy** to work longer than I already do to save more money for things that I want.

MONEY—I don't have the **money** to go on holiday. I don't have the **money** to spruce up the house. I don't have the **money** to put into a pension or investment plan.

PEOPLE—I don't know **anyone** who can help me. There is **nobody** to help with my kids. My **family** is not supportive of my dreams. My **friends** do not care about my goals. There is **no one** out there who can help me change my life.

Take a look at these excuses. Sound familiar? Have you found yourself using them? The truth is, we all use them. It's easy to shirk our responsibilities by ascribing our failures or lack of action to something else, real or imagined.

The good news is that you can take these TEMP excuses and make them TEMPorary. Recognize what you are doing (or not doing) and leave them behind. You have the power, the control, the influence over your life. You can take responsibility for yourself. Imagine being in the life you love, and then own it, influence it, and take action.

Self-Check

If you look at your life right now, are you on track for what you had imagined for it? Is the future you imagined for yourself, your family, and others within reach, or have you wandered off the chosen path or let roadblocks impede your progress?

Let's take a few minutes to truly assess where you are in life. Answer the following questions honestly so you understand where you are at this moment in your life.

The things in my life that I want to change are:

_____

_____

_____

_____

The things I believe I can directly change or influence are:

_____

_____

_____

_____

The first steps I can take to change these things are:

_____

_____

_____

_____

The things I cannot change are:

_____

_____

_____

_____

The reasons I cannot change these things are (what or who):

_____

_____

_____

_____

The first few steps I can take to overcome these challenges are:

_____

_____

_____

_____

Summary

It's a lot easier to *not* take responsibility for your life than it is to acknowledge you are the one with the power—you are the cause of everything that transpires in it, good and bad. It's also a lot easier to blame others when you fall short of expectations or are not motivated to make the change needed to create the life you want.

Many times, we see people who use the handy excuses for why their lives are not what they intended them to be, and we give in to those fallacies of not enough time, money, energy, or support from others. If you find yourself doing this, STOP. Take responsibility for your own life. Assess where you are, what you want, and then take the action necessary to create the life you imagine.

Review Questions for Assess and Access the Life You Imagine

1. What am I not taking responsibility for in my life that I need to?

2. What do I need to do to move forward and make this happen?

3. What else is stopping me from moving on to where I need to be?

CHAPTER 3:

DEFINE WHO AND WHERE YOU WANT TO BE

If you want to be happy, be.

—Leo Tolstoy

All of us have had occasions in our lives when we explored the "what ifs and if onlys." You may have spent hours comparing yourself to your peers, colleagues, family, and friends, asking: *How do I measure up? How fast or slow am I going? Am I keeping up with everyone else?*

How do you reach clarity on where and who you want to be? How do you improve the life you have?

The answer is to stand on one side of the valley and look across.

Where you are now, in this moment, cannot be changed in this moment. But what you want and where you want to be is waiting on the other side of the valley. What is in that valley—what you must cross to get to the other side—must be faced with courage, conviction, and concentration. You must identify what you truly need in life—and not what you think you need—and make the leap across.

You sometimes hear people talk about how to live *a* life you love because, for many people, there is no such thing as *the* life. Living a life we love best can't be quantified or qualified simply because we all have many choices in the way our lives can go, and those choices can turn out differently for different people.

Michelle's Story

Consider the story of Michelle.

When I was younger, I always imagined being a teacher, specifically a German teacher. I suppose I liked the idea of imparting knowledge and making a difference. Unfortunately, my conversations with career advisers had not unearthed the fact that I needed qualifications in two languages to pursue this dream. As I had dropped French earlier on in my schooling, I only had one language requirement. Still, that didn't stop me in my pursuit of wanting to go to university; I chose to look at courses that combined German and English literature instead.

My plan came to an abrupt halt upon getting my A level results: I had failed German! However, my determination to go to university was so great that I called all the universities to ask if I could be accepted in the German and English literature course without having passed my German A level. After many calls and many rejections, Sunderland University said it would accept me on the condition that I re-sit my A level at the same time as completing and passing my first year of the degree course. I snapped their hands off! I went on to pass my degree with a 2:2 with honours.

It was during my final year of university that I met my future husband. We eventually married and had a son. I always thought that although we went through the ups and downs that married life brings, we would be able to work things through and be together forever. So my world and everything I had envisioned went into complete breakdown when we split up. This had not been part of the plan! I went through a whole array of emotions: fear, upset, anger. Mostly, I felt like a complete failure. I had not thought that I would ever have gotten divorced or been a single mom. Everything went through my mind: What if I'd have said or done something different? What if he had done something different? *It wasn't easy. And amid all those thoughts, we had to create a new relationship as separated parents. We were both committed to making things as easy as we possibly could for our son, so we kept the conversations going, even when we didn't want to, and came up with new agreements and boundaries.*

A big worry for me was the house. What is going to happen now? Where were we going to live? *I didn't want to move. We had bought a house in a lovely area with a great community and wonderful schools. But on paper, the sums didn't add up. How was I going to buy my ex-husband out of the house and get a mortgage on my own? With Jaqui's coaching, I committed to keeping the house. It seemed impossible. I had no idea how I was going to do it. It took many conversations with financial people, my ex, and solicitors. I remember that one of the hardest conversations I had was with a financial person. I had to go through all my finances—everything— with him! I felt sick with worry. I was so nervous, I was scared, and I was* vulnerable. However, the contrast an hour after I walked out of that meeting was amazing. Not only did he tell me he'd seen worse, but he also assured me that he didn't think there would be a problem in organising a mortgage that covered everything. I was elated! A year after separating from my husband, I had bought him out of the house and the mortgage was in my name.

During the early stages of our separation, our son started to act out. He was four years old at the time and started hitting, kicking, and being really angry. I decided that I had to enrol him in something that would channel all his energy and aggression. I decided on martial arts as I believed in its ethos, teaching respect, discipline, and defence as well as providing fitness and confidence. I remember when I called to enquire about James joining. I was asked if I had ever thought about doing martial arts. I responded with a resounding, "No!" However, James and I went to the introduction together that night and then watched the family class that followed. We were hooked! There were fifteen belts to pass altogether—the fifteenth being the black belt—and we would discuss how great it would be to be black belts one day, even though that day seemed like a million years away.

We focused on each stage and each belt. We motivated each other. When I'd had a tiring day at work, James would say, "Come on, mum, I want to go to martial arts." I'd do the same when he was tired. The training for the actual black belt was like nothing we'd gone through before. Part of the grading was to run; James had to run 5km within forty minutes and I had to run 8km within fifty minutes. Not only did I wonder how I was ever going to be able to run that (given that I had not run since I was at school), but I was also consumed by the fear and worry of how my little six-year-old boy was going to be able to run 5km, a distance a lot of adults would struggle with, within that timeframe. Still, we faced it like we had everything else: We made a plan; had a lot of determination, grit, and persistence; and we kept our dream of being black belts at the forefront of our minds. In March 2009, two and a half years after starting our martial arts training, we both became black belts. James was six years old, and I was thirty-five.

When I look back, my life is not how I imagined it would be. Yet, in many ways it is so much better, so much more fulfilling. I have a great relationship with my ex-husband, so much so that I often find myself being a support and a help to him. That didn't just happen overnight. It has taken time, many conversations, and forgiveness, patience, and tolerance. Most of all, it has taken remembering that we have a beautiful son who deserves to have two parents in his life, whether they are together or not. My ex-husband and I want James to be happy, so we always keep that in the front of our minds.

So, what is next? Well, as someone who previously hated running but managed to do the 8km for my black belt grading, I thought it would be challenging *to run a half-marathon. So, that's my plan for the first half of 2010. James wants us to go for second degree black belts, which we are now in training for and will be grading for in a year's time. And, I'd like to fall in love again.*

Defining Happiness

As Michelle's story shows, life does not always work out the way we plan. However, she took responsibility for it. While she faced formidable challenges in school and her marriage, Michelle identified what she needed to do in her life (to be a teacher, to properly care for James), and took the necessary action to imagine a new life and, ultimately, find happiness (although she is still working on finding that new love).

Michelle is an example of someone who took control of her life amid hard times. She defined who she was and where she wanted to be in life. And that is something that you will need to do to strengthen your core being and create the life that will make you happy.

William Dempster Hoard, a nineteenth-century politician, probably put it best when he said "Happiness doesn't depend on what we have, but it does depend on how we feel toward what we have. We can be happy with little and miserable with much."

So to define where you want to be really comes down to this: What does happy *feel* like for you?

Does it have to do with the intangibles? Is it having a loving spouse, children, or significant other? Good friends who will be there for you through the good times and bad? Is it having more time to do the things you want? Is it having a sense of fulfillment and accomplishment?

Or does happiness for you manifest itself in material worth? Is it the fancy homes and exotic vacations? The expensive cars and jewelry? Is it the security of a robust bank account? It's true that many people do equate money with happiness, mostly for the lifestyle that wealth affords. Yet, here's an interesting finding from the London School of Economics regarding this. In a 2008 World Happiness Survey conducted by the school, researchers found that poorer countries were actually happier than richer nations. People from Bangladesh and Armenia, whose bank accounts pale in comparison to those in the United States and Britain, ranked higher for perceived happiness.

What do these findings point to? It would appear to confirm the old adage that money can't buy happiness. It can't buy "*the* life."

This brings us back to standing above the valley and looking across to see what you truly need in life as opposed to what you think you need. You'd be amazed at how we can make life very complex and confusing by wishing for things that actually have no real value to us. Usually, most people find that it's the basics that make them happy:

To be healthy

To be loved

To be financially secure

To be self-expressed

To be growing and learning

Now, you might say that what are basics for some people are huge—and even luxuries—for others. This may be so. We believe that people generally put their attention (and, therefore, actions) into what they are really committed to. It works in all areas: health (healthy lifestyle), love (being in a relationship), financial security (working or finding a way to pay for their lifestyle while not spending more than they actually have), self-expression (and spending time working in areas that suit their expression), and growth and development (by spending time and focus on areas that will contribute to claim ownership of their life).

Taking responsibility for your life begins with taking responsibility for your happiness. If you are prone to relinquish that responsibility to others, you are handing over your life to them. Your present and your future are dependent on them, not you.

The simple truth is this: Only you can make yourself happy. Let us repeat that: *Only you can make yourself happy.*

To be the cause in your life, you alone must define where you want to be and set on the path that will get you to the other side of the valley.

Being the cause in your own life requires you to be courageous, to face up to getting through the changes you will need to go through to cause yourself into your new future, your imagined future. People stop themselves from being the cause of their own lives because they see themselves as not quite ready for the changes or too frightened of the costs and consequences of changing. To affect change and to be the cause in your own life takes vision, knowledge, and a realization of the costs associated with creating a life you love.

The Change Equation

When you think you want to change and then find you are not taking the necessary steps to do so, look at this to help you to work out why that might be.

There is a resistance-to-change formula that was put together by Beckhard & Gleicher, and here is a similar version of that school of thought. The equation looks like this:

$$D > (V + K + C)$$

The D stands for the dissatisfaction with what you have going on in your life.

What is my dissatisfaction?

_____

_____

_____

The V stands for the vision that you have of what your life, or part of your life, might look like—the vision of the change you want to cause or create. If you have trouble creating a vision for yourself, then ask a friend to help you create one.

What is my vision?

_____

_____

_____

The K stands for the knowledge, or the first few steps, you need to take on the way to the new change. It is not the whole process but rather the first few steps of it. You may not have a clue about any of the steps, so you need to reach out to others and ask if they have any ideas about the steps you need to take to go about realizing your vision. While the vision can be sometimes hard to find, the knowledge can sometimes hold people back, especially when they think they must have it all worked out before they start causing the change.

My first few steps are:

_____

_____

_____

The C stands for the costs, or the consequences, of the new change. You may have to pay for something or you may have to disappoint someone with your new change, or you may have to quit something old for something new and that might be very confronting. The costs and the consequences are what often stop people from creating something new in their life.

The costs and consequences I see are:

_____

_____

_____

The dissatisfaction has to be much bigger than the vision, the knowledge, and the costs or the consequences put together for someone to get moving on creating and causing the changes they wish to see for themselves. If the dissatisfaction isn't big enough, then you are unlikely to take actions to change.

Am I dissatisfied enough to make new changes?

Here's an example:

We want a new home.

Vision—We can see a house for sale in the next village that costs $200,000 more than where we live now.

Knowledge—We talked to a financial advisor who gave us an idea of the cost of the mortgage for the new house and the deposit required. Our salary just covers the difference. It is tight, but we can manage it.

Costs and consequences—We will spend all our savings on making the new deposit. We will have to cut back on going out in the first two years of owning the new house. We may have to sell the second car to make the payments. We will have to sell the house we live in at present within a few months.

Now given all of the above—the vision, the knowledge, and the costs and consequences—are we dissatisfied enough with where we live now to take the action to buy the new house?

The Joy of Responsibility

Remember this about change: it takes effort and lots of it. It also takes serious consideration, as the choices you make could impact some or all areas of your life. Many people avoid change because it means stepping outside the comfort zone, moving into unfamiliar territories that test the very essence of their core. Taking full responsibility for your life will, without doubt, bring on change—new restrictions and boundaries, new paths, new people, and new focus that leaves little time for the sundry activities that have kept you from living the life you always dreamed.

However, taking responsibility for your life also brings with it one other thing: joy.

When you are the author of your life, you have the satisfaction of knowing that it is a life you have created. There is joy in knowing that all that is and can be is a direct result of you taking control of the reins. It is a joy in knowing that you are living the life you are meant to live.

We are most content with our lives when we are most happy. It seems a simple enough saying, but really think about it. Discontentment breeds anger and unhappiness that manifests itself in our areas of our lives. Contentment, on the other hand, engenders joy and happiness that translates to all areas of our lives—to our relationships with others, our commitment to work, our health, and our sense of place in the world.

You see examples of joyless people all the time, those who have left the decisions for their lives in the hands of others: the son who feels compelled to follow in his father's footsteps, the worker who allows an overbearing boss to force overtime on him, the woman who gives in to the demands of family and lets go of her dreams. These people, in effect, are assigning their lives to others. Is that a life you want? Are you content to let others shape your future?

While taking full responsibility for your life may seem like you are adding to your schedule and pressures, the joy you will discover in authoring your life will provide you with the energy and the enjoyment you need to overcome the perceived or actual obstacles. Knowing you are intentionally working toward a life you love will see you through the efforts required to achieve it.

Summary

In order to define who and where you want to be, you must first take stock of where you are now. This is the most critical step in imagining the life you want. You have to be completely honest with yourself—what are those things that will make you happy and what are the things that you only think will make you happy. You also have to dispense with the what ifs and if onlys. Acknowledge that life sometimes does not turn out as planned, and then move on.

Once you have done this, place your attention on what it is you wish to manifest in your life—what you can cause to change and what you can do immediately to affect that change.

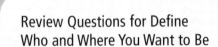

Review Questions for Define Who and Where You Want to Be

1. What do I truly need in my life?
2. What does happy look like for me?
3. What are the first steps?

CHAPTER 4:

CREATE A LIFELINE

Surround yourself with only people who are going to lift you higher.

—Oprah Winfrey

Now, we hope we have made the point that you are the cause of your life. You are responsible for the ups and downs, the good and bad, and the gains and losses. The direction your life takes is entirely dependent on the control you exert over the influences that can lead you from one side of the valley to the other.

However, we want to stress this point as well: While you alone are in control, you are not alone in the journey.

Sometimes, to get across that valley, you need a lifeline.

Seek Your Supporters

As much as we do come across those who will hold us back from our dreams—and you will come across both the vocal and subtle naysayers—most people really do want to see you happy. They do want to help you in your journey. Seek and take advantage of the help that is offered along the way.

How do you do this? It's as simple as getting a partner, or partners, who believe in your dreams and will support you in imagining all you can be.

Take a look at some of the greatest achievers in the world, those men and women who have ascended to great heights in business, medicine, sports, and politics. What do they all have in common? The answer is a support system that encouraged them and allowed them to pursue what others told them was impossible.

Andrew Carnegie was a poor Scottish boy who immigrated to the United States without a penny in his pocket yet dreaming of great wealth. He wound up the richest man in the world in the early nineteenth century. How did he do it? He created lifelines. He surrounded himself with people smarter than he who would help him learn the steel industry, and then he hired even smarter people to manage his business for him.

A hundred years later, Mary Kay Ash did the same thing. The national training director for a direct selling company in the early 1960s, Ash was passed over for promotion in favor of a man she had trained. Frustrated, she left the company and started her own. With the support of her son, second and third husbands (her second husband died before her first store opened), and business associates, Ash grew her company into Mary Kay Cosmetics Inc., a global leader in beauty products. Today, Ash is considered one of the greatest female entrepreneurs in American history.

Now, we're not saying that if you find some really smart and supportive people that you can become millionaires as well. The point here is that Carnegie and Ash were not only dreamers, they were doers because they had support mechanisms in place to keep them focused on their goals and to encourage their progress.

Let's bring the example down to earth for those of us who are not business geniuses. Take a look around you and you will see countless examples of achievers—from the student who thought they would never make it through school until a caring teacher stepped in to guide her steps . . . the athlete who never dreamed of making it to the Olympics until a coach instilled a winning belief in him . . . the mother who worried she would not be a good parent until her mother showed her the way.

There are people out there waiting to help you. All you have to do is connect with them. And here is the miraculous thing about making connections: There are no random meetings. You are in exactly the place you are supposed to be at the moment you are there. Your access to a life you love expands to an infinite degree as your connections expand. The more people of substance you know—people you connect to on the basis of their values and their integrity—the more likely it is that you will have a vast web of people who love and support you through your life.

Any number of people will help you along the way. There exists the idea that every person is connected by only six degrees of separation. With technology and travel today, the world has become a smaller place, and we are more apt to be about three degrees separated from anyone else in the world. The more people you know, the more connected you are to the information you need and the resources you require.

Candace's Story

Consider the story of Candace.

My biggest life interruption was not knowing or understanding what self-respect meant and choosing the wrong people in my life. I have since grown and learned about the responsibility of self-love and love for others. It's a daily growth!

As a child I was a victim of domestic violence, and I ended up being a street kid in Vancouver who eventually became a missionary's wife for two years during the implosion of apartheid. Now I speak on personal growth and encourage my audiences to take responsibility for their own success through the simple technique of the "3 R's™"—Doing the RIGHT thing, at the RIGHT time, for the RIGHT reasons.

I talk openly about my deeply intense life struggles with the ease of one who knows how to truly overcome. I believe that when you build the life of others, you automatically build yourself. I think sharing who you are requires a no-nonsense approach, and it doesn't hurt to be self-deprecating and have a good sense of humor. There is a lot of stuff that gets in the way in life, and I share my struggles to help others.

For example, my family has just survived three-and-a-half years of my granddaughter suffering from cancer. She was diagnosed at only fifteen months old. She is now five and a half, and a one-year cancer survivor! In times of strife, people must pull together, we must help each other. When there are obstacles, there are definitely opportunities. Just be the best you can be in the trying times.

My life is not what I imagined it would be in my childhood, but the way I have lived it has certainly been a conscious choice in the past ten years— although I didn't think or imagine that it could have gone this far! As a little girl, I simply imagined being a mother, wife, and entertainer! I sang a lot, was a comedian, and was very, very adventurous at a young age. Though I have been a singer and a songwriter, I now support others as they entertain the world. I have my own business (which I didn't imagine), and right now I am closer to my "being" than I have ever been!

For more than ten years, I have taught over 100 women a year in health-care disciplines and human relations. I have a diploma in The Provincial Instructors Program and over twenty years of experience in two health-care occupations. I am also responsible for writing and creating health-care-related curriculum currently being used in four adult education programs within three school districts, including three community colleges. I employ a "can do/will do" style and utilize my knowledge, my passion, and my no-fear networking skills to educate and provide resources, services, and products to women and their families—all in support of my goal to teach people to become part of the solution. I hope my experience inspires and gives hope and answers.

In my role as executive producer, I use my networking skills to make strong inroads in Hollywood. In one year alone, I connected and booked more than 660 guests and co-produced three primetime specials that received exceptional audience reviews. This ability to reach out beyond barriers is the key to building strong networks of relationships and resources, enabling the hosts to provide content-rich interviews for television. I continue to pitch shows to major stations and am responsible for networking and the signing of co-production deals.

Not bad for a street kid, huh?

I have only put one dream on hold—to tell my life story in a way that is uplifting to those that read it but not hurtful to those who have affected it. That is the only real dream that I desire . . . to use my life to encourage and strengthen others. Other than that, long ago I learned to live my life without regrets. I have pursued my passions and taken risks. It is good!

To a certain extent, I have accomplished what I wanted, although I would still like to accomplish gaining a reputation of being wise and excellent in my personal and business practices (long way to go). A wise old king once wrote "a good name is better to be chosen than great riches"; if you have a good name and people trust you, then you have true riches.

What's next for me is to be a woman who is invited into a trusted influence in high places and inner circles, to reach those that are normally protected in their inner circles and to serve them with love and compassion and build trust and friendship so I can, hopefully, add to their lives. Often, those in high places of influence can't trust those that speak to them or want to connect to them because they are uncertain of their intentions. I have nothing I want from them except to share with them some insights that might assist them in making the lives around them better. I want to write a book to show people how to truly use their power. I am learning this as I live right now!

Connections and Contacts

Candace is someone who has learned that creating lifelines helps you not only overcome life's struggles, but also simply reach out into the world and make the connections needed to help you imagine living the life you have imagined. Establishing relationships with people who are interested in your well-being and supportive of your goals can lift you during the low times and raise you even higher during good times.

If you are not doing so already, keep a database or a spreadsheet of all the people you know. You will be astounded at how large the number is and can be as you continue to make connections. Every time you make a new acquaintance, add the information to your database. It doesn't matter if you are a stay-at-home mom or a CEO: Keep your list of contacts and connections updated.

You will use these resources in your time of need as much as for invitations to parties or special events. You will also use this list when someone in your network approaches you with a request for help. There is no greater gift than to be able to introduce people you care for or respect so that they may support one another in the world. In fact, relationships make the world go round, and you already have a variety of types of relationships that you know you can utilize. Do yourself a favor and utilize them. Connection is key.

Now, with that said, remember that once you have identified or developed your lifelines, be sure to share with them your goals and dreams. No one knows what you need in your life unless you tell them. Let your lifelines know what it is you imagine being, and ask them to be there for you as a support system. When you are committed to take action for what you want in life, you may experience a feeling of uncertainty as to how and where to start. This is when your lifelines will be of the most help to you. Remember, very few people really achieve their dreams without a little, or a lot, of help from others. Don't let your ego or your fear stop you from reaching out. Turn off those little voices in your head that fill you with lines such as "I'm a failure"; "I'm incompetent"; "I'm weak or needy to let someone else help."

That is just crazy thinking. All the tough guys of the world and all the successful people who get what they want out of life rely on others to help them. Rely. Said again: *Rely* on others to help them.

Think about it: You rely on an electric company to pipe power into your home; you rely on pilots to fly you across country; you rely on journalists to keep you informed; you rely on doctors to take care of you. It's okay to rely on others to help you become all that you imagine being.

You can start the process of developing your lifelines by doing the following:

- Request that your lifeline help you review what is important to you in life. Be sure to cover all areas—family, career, faith, health, and whatever else is important and necessary for you to imagine being in the life you love.

- Talk to your lifeline about why the needs and wants are important to you.

- Write down the needs and wants and ask your lifeline for guidance in attaining them.
- Enlist your lifeline in helping you overcome any obstacles.

(For more information on engaging lifelines, refer to the workbook.)

As for obstacles, which we will cover later, do keep this in mind: When building your lifeline network, be careful who you choose. While many people will stand in line to help you, there are many others, even those close to you, who will try to stand in your way.

Let's face it, in the fast-paced world we live in, many people are vying for our time and attention. There may be family or friends who may influence how your time is spent—who keep you from pursuing what you truly desire. If the people in your lifeline network are not prepared to contribute to what you need, then you will be faced with a decision—keep control of your own life or turn that control over to them. What will you choose?

Summary

You are never alone in your journey. All around you are people ready and willing to help you. Take advantage of the support offered by others. Share your dreams with them, and let them help you stay committed to the plan you have put in place for your life. In doing so, you will be able to create a lifeline network that can help you through any situation.

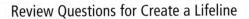

Review Questions for Create a Lifeline

1. Who are my support people—those who can help me imagine being?

2. What can I do now to create a database of contacts?

3. How can I reciprocate and be of service to others?

CHAPTER 5:

HOLD YOURSELF ACCOUNTABLE

It is not only what we do, but also what we do not do, for which we are accountable.

—Molière

Who is the cause of your life? You.

Who is responsible for your life? You.

Who needs to reach out to others for help? You.

Who is going to hold you accountable for becoming all that you imagine being?

Yes, you.

We are taught at an early age that we are accountable for our actions. It's a simple lesson that is instilled in us and never leaves. If we commit a transgression against another person, we will be called out for it. If we run up excessive bills on credit cards, we will have to pay the penalty. If we commit a crime, we will have to serve the time.

It's strange that the laws put in place to secure a free and safe society are, for the most part, abided by the citizens of the world, yet when it comes to holding ourselves accountable for our own lives—to secure our futures and realize our dreams—those laws are not only by and large ignored, but they are also . . . unwritten.

There are no guidelines to keep ourselves in check. There are no rules that say we have to be kind and giving to ourselves.

"Yes, I wanted to get in shape this year, but my work schedule is just too busy to find the time." "Yes, I wanted save up for that nice home by the lake, but I really wanted to try my luck in Vegas." "Yes, I wanted to go back to school to earn my degree so I could get a better job, but I'm just so tired after work."

When it comes to us and what we want and need, we are long on good intentions and short on action. It's far too easy to put off all those spectacular dreams, infinite possibilities, and boundless energy that would fully allow us to participate in life, to live a life *with* purpose and *on* purpose.

Nobody is going to stand over you and force you to pursue that life you want. That's why it is critical that you hold yourself accountable for all you do.

Later in this book we'll talk about declaring intentions and writing a plan for your life, but you must first understand the importance of accountability. It is the keystone of a life filled with purpose.

Accountability manifests itself in everything—from the relationships you nurture, to the food you put in your body, to the decision to stay in shape, to the strict adherence to goals set, to the completion of action items.

While the lifelines you develop will support you in your efforts and help hold you to the commitments you have made, the person who will ultimately decide whether you are making progress toward the end goal is you. You alone are accountable for what happens in your life. Not your spouse. Not your children. Not your boss. You. You are both judge and jury, and you must have the strength and courage to come down hard on yourself if you are falling short of expectations.

It's a tough job. It's not easy to stave off the excuses that are waiting nearby for the tiniest of openings. But you have to do it.

So how do you? Here's one way: box yourself in, to box yourself out.

Box In, Box Out

What do we mean by that? Boxing yourself in can happen at two levels: the day-to-day and the transformational. It may be easy to declare some of our intentions (boxing in), but without putting ourselves in the position of getting leverage to accomplish them (boxing out), they will fall by the wayside.

Day-to-day boxing yourself in includes putting the heat on yourself regarding those intentions that are not typically one-time happenings but rather those that require attention regularly. The idea is to box yourself in by declaring your intention publicly to a supporter, or to engage a legal or medical practitioner in the mix. For instance, if you want to lose ten pounds, ask one of your lifelines to be present at your weigh-ins or go to the doctor's office and have a nurse supervise and write your result (or lack thereof) in a file. You can box yourself in by hiring a trainer, a financial advisor, a relationship coach, or a business consultant. Often, a method of boxing yourself in is to put some skin in the game. If you have a financial commitment, you will be less likely to shirk your responsibility and squander your money.

Transformational boxing yourself in can lead to instant or large-scale change that requires adjustment to the immediate challenges you've instigated and now need to overcome. This level of boxing yourself in is a choice you make that does not include the path of least resistance, but the one less traveled. For example, in moving to the San Diego area, Kristin had to ensure she made $2,000 more per month than she was already earning in order to make ends meet. While it may not seem like a large amount of money, she still had to find a way to achieve that goal. She did not have it figured out before she moved 2,000 miles to the "Left Coast," but she did not let it interfere with her decision to go. She put herself in the position of needing to expand her network and client base quickly, and hit the ground running to establish herself in the new environment.

By boxing yourself in, you are forced to put up your dukes and box your way out. By self-inflicting the boxing in, you are forced to figure out how to overcome the obstacle you've created. This simple act of defiance on your part results in filling you with a sense of empowerment that you can meet any of life's challenges head on—and win!

Here are some other ideas for holding yourself accountable:

- Promise a lifeline that you will send a monthly progress report (and suggest they do the same to keep the balance).

- Declare your intentions publicly (with some tact and appropriateness, of course).

- Keep your plan in front of you wherever you are.

- Read, learn, and grow around the areas of your intentions. Discover the experts and model yourself after them. Put yourself in the way of inspiration and motivation.

- If you have always wanted to 'do' something or go somewhere, schedule the event or trip and place your attention on figuring out the balance. There's no time like the present to transform your life.

There will be times when you set down a path only to discover it is not what you thought it would be. In such instances, it's not a matter of when the tough get going but that the smart realize they've miscalculated their intentions. Just remember that it's okay to change course. Don't stay on it merely because you told people you would or that you're concerned about their perception of your ability to follow through. And . . . don't let yourself off the hook either. (We will discuss more about Course Corrections later.)

It is, after all, your life. If it's not working, change it. But when you do, hold yourself accountable for the new course, and you'll find that the end result is much more of what you imagined it being.

Summary

While others will be there to support you on your journey, the one person who is completely accountable for your life is you. In taking responsibility for your life, you are the one that ultimately holds yourself accountable for all your actions—or lack thereof.

Practice boxing yourself in for those areas of your life that need your attention, whether it be business, relationships, or health. It may be difficult at times, but the empowerment you will feel in boxing your way out of those seemingly hard situations will allow you to face any challenge ahead.

Review Questions for Hold Yourself Accountable

1. How can I box myself in to help ensure I keep myself on track toward my intention?

2. Is there a person or coach who can monitor my progress with me?

3. What things do I need to stop doing, and what things do I need to start doing?

4. What is one thing that I've wanted to do in my life that I've been putting off to tomorrow?

5. What will I do right now to box myself in so I achieve it?

PART TWO:

IMAGINE BEING THE OPPORTUNITY

It is not in your environment,
it is not in luck or chance, or the help of others;
it is in yourself alone.
Orison Swett Marden

No great man ever complains of want of opportunity.
Ralph Waldo Emerson

It is our choices that show what we truly are, far more than our abilities.
J.K. Rowling

In this section, you will learn to:

- Take advantage of the Big O
- Be the author of your life
- Reject the "ah buts"
- Declare your intentions
- Identify your Super Champions
- Write your plan
- Play your choice cards

CHAPTER 6:

OUR OPPORTUNITIES

*T*here is a saying that if you can imagine it, you can do it. Your imagination creates opportunities, and your opportunities are limited only by your imagination. Have you heard of millionaire thinking? The cogs of your brain are sometimes limited by what you think is possible. If you grew up impoverished, to reach millionaire status may seem like a very distant possibility. Though if you expand your imagination to really believe that whatever you imagine can become real, you can cause the opportunity in your life and the lives of others.

You will begin to realize that the possibilities for your life and your contributions in the world are whatever you choose to create. Then once you begin to "dream," you must attain focus. Letting your imagination run wild is exactly what you should do—once it has galloped through sea, desert, and land—rein it in and really focus on what you imagined, and then how you will make it possible.

Creating opportunities is not a difficult task. You must be willing to put yourself out there. What feels like a risk is likely not that much of a risk at all. Better to have tried and been turned down than not to have tried.

Kristin's Story

In August, eight months after I'd undertaken KristinFest (the celebration of a year past and defining my intentions for the new year), I went home to visit my mom and dad. It was at my mom's house that

I had an "I wish I would have" conversation with myself. I had not accomplished a fraction of my intentions. A trip to Bermuda had rolled around and there was no fit body. Tax time came, and my finances had me panicked. Three months had passed from the last visit to my parents, breaking my "every eight weeks" promise. I'd moved to California nearly a year ago and still had not joined organizations or met people. There was no man manifested in my life. So I realized that I'm writing a book with my dear friend on a subject at which I have failed, time and again, year after year...

And yet, I am aware that I am succeeding more so than if I had not given this process conscious thought and attention.

After this realization of my "status quo self," I shifted into high gear, and the successes happened in rapid fire. I woke one morning counting my seven new friends. (I'm serious, I did actually take satisfaction in counting them.) I declared my intention to grow my business and piled up seven new clients, more than doubling my monthly income. I made the next plan to visit home. I hoped to lose the weight and feel fit . . . and fumbled on that one, yet again. Yep, I'm human.

So am I happy? More often than not.

I accomplished a lot in short order, and I learned this, too: I was in action, though more to check the accomplishments off my list than with an eye on fulfillment. I was the perpetual human do-er. Not necessarily bad, but no sense in getting in the hamster wheel. This life is meant to be enjoyed. Shame on me if I get caught up in the busy-ness and forget to take the time to pause, step outside, and give thanks for the gifts of my life . . . as it is right now, in this very moment.

How does opportunity begin? When I lived in Springfield, Illinois, I was just launching my business. I was pretty broad with my service offerings. I focused on what I knew how to do, but not necessarily what I loved to do. I had bills to pay. I began expressing to people that I wanted to participate in good work—work that contributed to the lives of others and, perhaps specifically, to young people. I joined business women's organizations and the Chamber of Commerce, and would let people know of my interest in this contribution. I met a person who suggested that I contact Stedman Graham.

Frankly, at that time, I didn't know who Stedman was or what he did. I learned quickly that he had written two *New York Times* bestsellers (among his many books), one of which was specifically directed toward teens (*Teens Can Make It Happen—A Nine-Step Plan for Success*). Through the person who knew him, I obtained a meeting. Prior to that meeting, I prepared a PowerPoint proposal titled, "Kids Can Make It Happen." We drove to Chicago and entered his office. This giant of a graceful man entered the conference room, which overlooked Lake Michigan and Navy Pier, and after quick introductions, I launched into the presentation. He sat beside me looking at the computer screen and listening. When I finished, he said he didn't want to do what the presentation suggested, but he liked how I put it together and how I delivered it—and asked how we could work together. That was in 2003, and we are still working together.

My philosophy in life is that anything is possible, everyone is accessible, and we are all connected. If you want to create opportunity in your life:

Be clear on your reason, and ensure your intention is pure.

Prepare to communicate with the people who may help you and who you want to be in opportunity with. Do your research and offer value.

Give it your best shot, and don't give up.

Let go of the outcome. If you receive a "no," it was not meant to be. Get on to the next!

On my wish list of people to work with are two individuals who I look up to and whose work I respect to my core: Tony Robbins and Bono. I know . . . perhaps a bit night and day in terms of how they line up with one another, but two people who have made a conscious choice to serve in this world on a global stage. I greatly respect people who utilize their influence and their access for the well-being of others, and these two have chosen to do so on a grand scale. Imagine how many people I could serve in partnership with their efforts. Now while my philosophy is that everyone is accessible, the truth is that it's not always that easy. Both Robbins and Bono have quite a few layers of people to get through before you can get to them. And the reason for communicating with them can certainly not be about celebrity or fame. The intention must be pure, and the proposition must be unique, valuable, and aligned with what they are up to in the world.

Therefore, while my intention is to meet, serve, and work with Bono, for example, I will have to exercise my network to find a common connection. I must find a way to let him know I am invested in his humanitarian work and impressed with his sensibility in using his celebrity to support causes. I believe in my core that an opportunity to meet him will arise, and I will persevere until it does as I am pulled to serve people who are currently not able to serve themselves.

Jaqui's Story

It was July 2009, five years after my husband and I had declared our intention to own a vacation home in Mallorca, Spain. We chose Mallorca—a beautiful Mediterranean island measuring 3,640 kilometers with a population of 790,000—as the place we could use for several weeks of the year for now, and for half the year in our more senior years.

The idea to look for property in Mallorca first came in 2004. My mum had taken ill, and during her long decline we had taken a vacation, where we had seriously reviewed our lifestyle and questioned what was life really all about. We decided that life was certainly not about working too hard. About acting like a hamster on a wheel. About being too busy with life and not taking time out to reflect. We had been working long hours while noticing the fragility of my mum and the unpredictable nature of life.

So we had found a frontline apartment in a new development in Mallorca, and we thought we had found our dream place. However, in the process of purchasing the property—as we were signing cheques in the notary's office—we found inconsistencies in the agreements and chose not to seal the deal. It was heartbreaking.

Then, in July 2009, we found ourselves looking again for that idyllic spot in beautiful Mallorca. This time, we found a little house in a fishing village and chose, once again, to go for it! It took a lot to make it happen. We had only a small amount of money to make the deposit, and you need to allow for an extra 10 percent of the purchase price for the taxes. Even though property prices were falling in mainland Spain in the midst of the global recession, the market in Mallorca remained the same. Eventually, the developer agreed to a 20 percent discount on the price, in addition to the 10 percent reduction they had already made on the list price.

We were still struggling to meet the workable numbers to purchase the property when the agent agreed to give up some of his commission to encourage the sale. When we were satisfied we could purchase the house, we returned home to find that within the previous week, the bank had changed its lending criteria. Even though we had agreed with the bank on the amount we could borrow the day before we went out to view properties, it had all changed. We chose to talk with the bank and request that it reconsider in light of its previous agreement. We were delighted when it chose to honour its original offer.

During July and most of August, there were weekly setbacks with regard to progressing the purchase, and we frequently questioned ourselves with respect to whether it would be worth all the hassle. Anyone who has bought a house knows how stressful it can be, and buying one in another country can be even more difficult. Every time we came across a setback, we wondered whether to continue, if it was worth the time, energy, and cost of going through with it all. Mostly what kept us both going ahead with it was the vision of what life would be like in the future—to live in a pretty place by the sea, the warm sunshine to enjoy most days of the year and a more relaxed lifestyle to look forward to, especially in our later years.

Of course, there was an even greater consideration throughout the entire process: Most of our life's savings was at stake, and we began to get a bit jumpy about whether it really was a wise move to make. Again, the lifestyle vision we had was mostly keeping us on track and on purpose in fulfilling our commitment. We came to realize that we may make a wrong turn, and we may lose money; though we had lost some sleep and peace of mind on the journey, this was temporary. The short-term setbacks, we believed, would generate a long-term fulfilling future.

When you set out to do things that are beyond your present experience, you can be quickly confronted with the uncertainty and the unknown. We all like to know or have some sense that everything is going to be okay. We often like to feel that we are in control of what is happening or what will happen. The thing is that in the complex, changing world we live in, it is hard to control much at all. Frequently, we find ourselves having to adapt and change according to what life throws at us.

I believe that being intentional isn't simply about getting what you want and making things happen the way you want them to happen. I believe that by intending something to happen while being flexible in the way in which you make it happen allows you to feel freer around the setbacks and issues along the way.

There are some that would point to the "ah but" you didn't do it in 2004 or the "ah but" you didn't buy it in the exact spot you said you were first looking. My response to this is: When you set a goal or an intention, do you then have to become a slave to it, just because you said it was that? I do not believe in becoming a prisoner of my intentions. My goals and intentions are there to support me and not to make me feel bad or close down other choices as time moves on.

Throughout life we all get pinged by unexpected events and setbacks. The more we can think through the possible setbacks, the better we will handle them when they arrive. However, no matter how much I look at this, I cannot account for all of the setbacks that may happen in my life. When the unexpected happens, I need to be as flexible and adaptable as I can possibly be.

Summary

Most of the time, when the unexpected setbacks come, we automatically respond with: "Oh, no! This should not be happening to me!" The thing is, it has happened, and now you need to deal with it. Life's events ping you with the unexpected, and it is up to you to handle them as efficiently as possible. When we allow the setbacks to ruin our day, we have lost power over how the day is going to go and how the situation will be handled. We become merely the victim of the setback.

Life is full of disappointments, and true freedom is found in our power to deal with the setbacks, find ways to move on from them, and get back on track with our quest to live a more fulfilling life.

Imagine being the opportunity maker in your life—and in the lives of others. Once you learn to take advantage of the opportunities you create, or with which you are presented, and as you author your intentions around them, you will need to address your doubts or excuses and have a game plan to accomplish what you set out to imagine being.

CHAPTER 7:

TAKE ADVANTAGE OF THE BIG O

We are all faced with a series of great opportunities brilliantly disguised as impossible situations.

—Charles Swindoll

---

*I*t is time to become 100 percent responsible for your own life. So often, we believe that life happens to us. Believe us, time will pass and life will happen. You could do what you've always done and get what you've always got, and 365 days from now be having the same conversation with yourself. In some cases, as with tragedy, life does happen. It is true that this is typically outside of your control. What you can manage, of course, is your response to it. There's nothing out there that says, "Hey, your life will be without problems." Every human has problems, and the intensity is relative, defined by each individual. Looking from the outside in at another's life, we will often say, "I want that," "I wish I was her or him." But, they have their stuff, too. Quit looking at *them* . . . turn the attention to YOU. Life encompasses the experience of death and of "I'm not good enough" conversations of boredom or unhappiness with yourself or others. This is just what is so.

Take advantage of the opportunity to learn from the experiences that result in your emotional or even professional growth. There is the old adage that says: When one door closes, another window opens. You need to be present to the possibilities of the opportunities that await.

It is also true that you have the opportunity to create joy, to give, to grow, to love, to become . . . to take the reins on your thoughts, deeds, and actions. Take advantage of the opportunity to create more of a life you love.

You can wait for life to happen and pass you by, or you can be deliberate about the outcomes you wish to manifest. You get but one turn in this life. We suggest you make the most of it. Learn that life is not a race . . . but that you cannot take it at an amble either.

First, you will need to clearly define what a life you love looks like for you. Then you will need to have a mindset and the know-how to cultivate the opportunities that create it. We will help to expand your thinking about the opportunities possible for you to create. We all get stuck in what we know, and we need perspective about how to explore our ability to think and dream big. We want your life to be riddled with opportunities, and will share examples of how to overcome limited thinking. We will move along to helping you define what you want, why you want it, and how you will go about achieving it. After you have nailed that, we'll provide methods for holding you to account.

As Tina Turner once said: "Sometimes you've got to let everything go—purge yourself. If you are unhappy with anything—whatever is bringing you down, get rid of it. Because you'll find that when you're free, your true creativity, your true self comes out."

So what is opportunity? Here is one definition:

Opportunity = a possibility due to a favorable combination of circumstances

There are many examples of people creating their opportunities. Some of the opportunities are small, as with the little girl with the lemonade stand in front of her house who is trying to earn money for her "horse fund." There are large-scale opportunities as well, as with the people who are reaching for their dreams through participation in reality TV shows. The odds of success may not be great, but even so, they give it a try.

And, there are the opportunities created by the entrepreneur who steps out on faith and starts a business. There are opportunities within your own home—to create a reading, writing, or painting room to inspire you. There are opportunities in the moment, right now, that require you to make an immediate choice. In the coming chapters, we'll explain the "choice cards" you have to play.

YOU create your opportunities and are responsible for them. Even if someone else offers an opportunity, you are responsible for drawing it to you. How you show up in the world can result in massive opportunity or missed opportunity.

Often, we see our circumstances as the saboteurs of opportunity, when they can actually be the cultivators of it, if framed properly. Notice, too, that *circumstances* is plural. One action does not necessarily mean you will have a life you love. You must set in motion a series of actions—capitalizing on a series of circumstances—and thus creating your own opportunity.

Circumstances + Action = Opportunity

(or Circumstances + Inaction = Stagnancy, Doldrums, a Ho-hum Life)

Think about the opportunities in your life. If you want an opportunity, create it. If you want to meet someone or do something, deliberately put yourself in the way of him, her, them, or it. Literally step onto the path and create the commotion that results in you owning the opportunity.

What are you willing to do to have a life you love? Are you willing to create your own opportunities? Remember that an opportunity can present itself in many ways. It can be in the form of an event that positively affects the outcome of a set goal or objective; in a favorable circumstance, such as advancement in your career or breakthrough in your work; or in a risk-related event.

Interestingly, opportunity may be hard to find because it can be difficult to define what we want out of life. Obstacles that get in the way are typically the games we play in our head (we call these the "ah buts," and will get to these later). They are the mind games that say:

+ "I don't deserve that."

+ "Even if I wanted it, I have no idea how to manifest it in my life."

+ "I'm scared."

You can endeavor to change, or you can create change. You can step up to the next curve, making the most of your current circumstances by changing how you approach life and work. You can take the fork in the road, making the most of your current circumstances by choosing something significantly different than what you have done for a good part of your life.

Ask yourself this: Can I make this stuff of life feel less like work and more like what I envisioned life was supposed to be?

How can I do that? Who can help? What will I do first, next, next? When will I make this happen?

Sit with those thoughts for a bit. Really think about them. And then frame this question in your mind:

"On this date _____, one year from today, what will my world look like?"

How will you cultivate your opportunities? At some point—why not today—you will be led to loosen your grip, stand your ground in the present, and point your chin to the future. Face the world head on and ask, "What's next?" And then, bring it on.

Summary

Your opportunity in life boils down to this: Your belief that all things are possible, that you have within you all that you need. Your life is personally within your power.

It's all you imagine being.

Review Questions for Take Advantage of the Big O

1. What opportunity do I desire?

2. What are the ways that I know of creating the opportunity for myself?

3. Who else can assist me in creating the opportunity?

4. If there were no limitations, what opportunities would I seek for myself?

5. What opportunities have I imagined that I have not taken because of the fear or concern for the risk that it is?

6. What are the opportunities I see for others where I can contribute?

CHAPTER 8:

BE THE AUTHOR OF YOUR POSSIBILITIES

Fill your paper with the breathings of your heart.

—William Wordsworth

*C*reate your life by design, not by chance. Living a life you love includes being the author of the design of your life, complete with clear intentions.

Being the author of your possibilities means you get to create and tell the stories of your life. The story you tell yourself can be one of "I can do it" or one of "I can't." The choices you make about your story will change the trajectory of each day and impact your life across your lifetime. Imagine the tales you can tell. Imagine the adventures you can cultivate. Imagine the contribution you can be and the love you can have and share. Imagine living in the life you love. Every day, you have the opportunity to author a new chapter in the book of your life.

Many of us face the same dilemma of not being sure what our possibilities or our intentions are. And, once we know them, we do not always know what to do next. In answer to the question, "What are the key 3–5 things you would like to know about having a life you love," a friend answered with the following:

- ◆ Figuring out what I love
- ◆ Then figuring out how to go after what I love

- Believing I deserve the life I want

- Understanding that it's okay (and helpful) to ask others for help

- Holding myself accountable

That, in a nutshell, is what we want you to be able to be, know, do, and think about. And it probably sounds familiar. But before we set you down the path of declaring your intentions, we would like to change the meaning of giving lip service to your intentions. From this point forward, LIP service is forever more defined as *Living in Possibility*.

Betty's Story

Consider the story of Betty.

Life isn't always easy, but it's possible to live a good life and a happy one. It sure wasn't easy for me in the beginning. My parents, three siblings, and I lived in a farmhouse between Milton and Time—population next to nothing—in Pike County, Illinois. We had very little. Mom had a bad heart and one of my sisters had been crippled with polio at age three.

I was told that mom was bedridden through much of her pregnancy with me. My sisters attended school while she stayed home, and they said one day their teacher tied a sugar sack to the saddle horn of the horse they rode to school. When the girls returned home, they delivered it to mom, who opened it. Tears rolled down her cheeks as it was filled with new baby clothes the local ladies had made.

I envision my mom being tender of heart, grateful and touched by others' kindness. That's what I envision; I never actually saw her. I was delivered at home by the doctor in December, and mom was taken by wagon to a hospital miles away. She passed three weeks later.

I listened to stories about my mom often, mostly those told by my grandmother, my older sister, and my aunt. My father was devastated by the loss of mom, and he moved out of our house. My grandmother took in the eldest kids—who were then five, seven, and nine—and I moved in with my Aunt June Helm and my uncle. I loved living with them. They pretty much became my parents. They had two sons who became brothers to me—and a buggy horse named Babe.

When I was younger, I imagined being a boy. I just wanted to do all the things boys could, like going with Dad (Helm) in the covered wagon to trade horses. I was told this was not a fit place for a little girl to be, but I loved that covered wagon! The inside of it was paneled with little shelves for medicines, and when Dad Helm came home he would put the cover in the yard and I had a playhouse! It was the greatest playhouse in the world. The bed was built in, and my doll babies could lay on it.

I loved my aunt and uncle. But when I was eight, my true father remarried and gathered all his kids together to live with him again on the farm. I was pretty traumatized by the move. I loved the Helms, and I ended up crying myself to sleep every night after I left. Without my playmates and familiar surroundings, I turned to reading, and I imagined being part of stories like Little Women, which I read at least fifteen times.

When I was about eleven years old, I decided that I didn't really want to be a boy. I thought, "I've got the world by the tail. Who do you think really, really rules the world? Women raise the sons that grow up to be presidents. I want to be a girl!" The only thing I ever really dreamed of was having the best husband in the world and a long, long happy marriage with a bunch of kids. And that's exactly what I got!

I married Glen in 1942 when I was sixteen. My dad had gotten sick and then had a heart attack, so Glen was hired to work on our farm. He lived with us all summer. The men at the local store said that I would be getting in trouble, but dad said Glen was a fine boy—but if it turns out I got pregnant, he'd love me just the same.

Glen went into the Navy, and I followed him to San Diego when I was eighteen. I arrived by bus and ended up sleeping in the bus station, at a church, and at a brothel—my sister-in-law and I did not know it was a brothel!—until finding proper rooms. When Glen came home after the war, we started our life together. We were dirt poor, but we didn't care. We were so happy together. We ended up having five children—Terry, Linda, Rick, Lynette, and Lori. I miscarried twice, too. What saw me through those life interruptions was my faith in God, and my great love for my husband and the children I already had.

Though we didn't have much, Glen and I took many trips with the kids. We saved all of our money, and any time it accumulated, we were off on the road in an old pop-up camper. We would put a card table up every night, light a lantern, and read and talk around it. If it rained, we played games with the kids under the table. Those were good times. We didn't have very many clothes, so we had to go to the laundromat every two days, and when we were hungry we'd stop and eat canned food off the back of the truck.

Glen and I spent every minute we could together. We especially loved carnivals and picnics. He passed of cancer a few years ago, after fifty-four years of marriage. I guess I attribute our success to simply loving each other. We both came from laid-back families that never fought or screamed at each other. We didn't think people did that, and I, at least, was more mature than most sixteen-year-olds because I'd had many things happen in my life by that time. We just loved each other 100 percent.

We lived in the moment, too. We thought anything was possible. Glen and I never thought about having anything on hold. We always made it, although I admit we were scared to death at times. But we always made it.

I never had much in the way of material things, but I have been rich in the things that matter most. I learned very young to accept things the way they were and adjust. And, I applied all this to the rest of my life. I knew I had to be satisfied with the wonderful things I had in my life.

I am eighty-four years old. I am happy. I've had a wonderful life. I haven't done anything very important, but I've loved the Lord and my family. I've loved many other people. The greatest gift is love. I don't have any money, but I don't care. I can't take it with me, anyway.

My life is better than I could have imagined it would be. I just wish Glen could be here.

Living in Possibility

You might think in reading Betty's story that her life was defined by tragedy—the death of her mother, the separation from her siblings, the trauma of leaving the Helms, the times of little or no money, and the miscarriages. Yet, according to her, she lived a rich life. How is that possible? For all she didn't have, Betty had one thing that many of us today are lacking—the ability to live in possibility. Throughout all the setbacks, Betty believed in a good and happy life, and she took the opportunities available to her to author the life of her choice—the happy marriage, the healthy children, and the family trips that created long-lasting memories.

Living in possibility means that you will be better equipped to take on transformational change.

Transformational change is different from incremental change because it usually requires you to think, behave, and act in a totally different way from how you may have acted and behaved today or yesterday. Transformation usually goes against what you see or believe is possible for yourself and others. The thought of transforming yourself can leave you quite worried and cold. It takes courage and a strong will to take on the big changes. Living in a transformed life will alter the way you act and behave. It has to, or there would be no transformation. This is likely to cause some discomfort at first as you get used to being and acting different to how you acted normally.

Here is an example from Jaqui's story:

I remember losing forty-two pounds and how I had to have a strong will and strong discipline to do it. I had to act and behave differently. There was incremental change involved in losing two pounds a week, and there was also a transformation of my eating habits. The slimming plan I was on required me to not eat anything and only drink water for five hours between meals. I had a history of snacking between meals and only ever going four hours between meals if I could help it. I remember once being on a train journey and wanting to eat my scarf—it seemed very tempting as I had another two hours to go before I could eat! I also transformed the way I put a meal together, replacing the carbs with a lot of good vegetables. I also drink a lot less alcohol, and now enjoy the alcohol when I actually do drink it.

Real transformation requires the following:

1. A willingness to invite some unknowns and find paths and ways of getting to know them.

2. The courage to stop doing some things that you did in the past and start doing new things now.

3. A good enough reason to want to transform. If you have no big reason, then you are unlikely to bother to change so much.

4. A willingness to reach out to others and ask for help from them, and accept the offers when they do.

5. The courage to talk through the impact this will have on the lives of others that are close to you, if there is a likely impact.

6. The discipline to use the new behaviors when you just want to go back to your old habits and behaviors.

7. The focus on the intention and the outcome you want to achieve. Keeping that at the forefront as much as possible.

8. A plan to get you there and a desire to share the plan with others (to be reviewed regularly).

Let's begin living in possibility:

• What did you dream about being or doing as a kid?

• What do you dream about as an adult?

• What do you know how to do? What are you good at?

• What makes you happy?

There is nothing you cannot do or be . . . you are up to anything you want to be in the world. Pay this idea LIP service! If you tell yourself you can, you can. This is proven and written in any number of publications (see the appendix for more resources). Live by this belief system and your life will bear the fruits of doing so. Don't live by that belief system and your life will labor with the status quo—or die on the vine. It is a matter of mediocrity or magnificence.

What do you believe is possible? Did you believe in Santa Claus as a child? Did you ever make a list of gifts for Santa Claus to bring you at Christmas? Be your own Santa Claus. Create your own presents. Let's start broadly:

• What do I want?

• How do I want to invest my time?

• What skills and talents do I have?

- What unique things can I do or say to make this day memorable for me and others?
- How can I alter my approach?
- How can I make a living doing and being something and someone I love?
- How can I make the most of this day? Tomorrow? The next?

You can ask these questions of yourself every day. Your answers may change based on where you are in your journey. To be the author of your possibilities, maintain an ongoing discussion with yourself and others regarding what is possible. Expand your thinking every day. Think outside the box, and read the stories of people who are succeeding in moving toward or living in the life they love. Live in your possibility.

If you choose them, the best times go on and on. The good news is, they are not hard to find. The bad news is, finding them is up to you. You alone are the author of your possibilities.

Summary

Pay LIP Service to your dreams. Believe that all things are possible and that you, as the author of your possibilities, are capable of making the transformational change needed to create the life you imagine living.

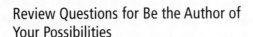

Review Questions for Be the Author of Your Possibilities

1. What do I believe is possible?
2. What possibilities will I author for myself?
3. If I could transform myself and my life, how would I feel each day?

✦ CHAPTER 9:

DECLARE YOUR INTENTIONS

Let your intentions be good—embodied in good thoughts, cheerful words, and unselfish deeds—and the world will be to you a bright and happy place in which to work and play and serve.
—Glenville Kleiser

We all have *desires*. Desires are like daydreaming—we go off into some shiny, magical wonderland. Desires are not, in themselves, intentions. It is only when you add action to the desire that it then becomes an intention, and often this starts with a *plan*. You look at what you think you want and then you plan for the actions to take accordingly.

You become intentional when you start acting out your dreams. Without action, there is only dreaming. You should also be aware that you may come up with BS intentions, those intentions that you are creating usually from the place of coulda, woulda, shoulda. You will notice if you have a BS intention quite quickly. How? You won't take action. When you notice yourself not taking action, look yourself in the mirror or talk to a friend and ask yourself, "Why I am not taking action?" Is it:

A) Because I am not committed fully to the life I said I wanted.

B) I've chosen an intention because it will make me please others, but I really could personally care less about it.

C) I cannot rely on myself to make it happen and need someone to help me.

Get it straight: Either you are going to make this happen for yourself, or you are not. If you need help, then say so, and start talking to people about it.

Taking Action

Declaring your intentions is about what you are creating and intending for your imagined life. It is one of the startup actions that is required and necessary. How do you clarify your intentions?

First, you have to place focused attention on assessing your intentions. It's easy to say "I want to lose weight" or "I want to be in a relationship." It's also easy to fall back on what you know—a comfortable place. You should know now that when you endeavor to change, you instigate chaos in your life. You put into motion a ripple effect of thoughts and actions that can throw you off center, and because it will take your attention and effort, you give it up. You will default to the things that you know. You will need leverage on yourself and you'll need the toolkit to manage setbacks.

Examples of common intentions:

- Healthy—lose weight
- Love—find a life partner
- Financial—spend less than I have and gain more than I have now
- Self Expression—change jobs

Examples of less common—perhaps transformational—intentions are:

- Live in San Diego
- Buy a house in Mallorca
- Begin a non-profit aimed at educating children
- Volunteer in South Africa
- Pay for a nephew's college tuition
- Change careers

All change requires effort, and transformation requires real effort. It requires you to be really flexible, adaptable, and unstuck from your normal ways of acting and responding in the world and with others. There will be all sorts of issues and worries that fly into your head as you think about all the effort it will take.

You'll also have to think how it will impact others, too. People can get very concerned about how a big change will impact those around them, and quite often, this stops them from taking change on. Granted, others will be affected at times, but you will have to talk the new changes through with them. Usually they are up for the change as much as you are, or you find a workable solution together.

Let's use an example of what we mean by this—changing jobs. All that you knew about how to do your current job becomes a thing of the past. You must now adapt to new ideas about a set of new circumstances as well as a new environment. You may not know exactly how to act and behave in the new circumstances, and this may require you to reach out to others for guidance. Transformational changes, as with career transitions, are riddled with the unknown and scary. However, there is a surprising amount of help available. People will step up to help you step into your transformed life.

Declaring your intentions is much like a declaration of independence—independence from the thoughts holding you back that limited thinking and inaction. Declaring your intentions is much like declaring your freedom—the freedom from an unfulfilling job, freedom from financial worries, and freedom of thought. Freedom is claimed from within. You will experience the feeling of freedom when you are in balance with what you need in life as a whole. If you really work at those areas that are important to you and take all the actions accordingly, you will experience the feeling of freedom.

Writing Your Intentions

Now, you need to create the statement of your intentions so that you are able to clearly describe your possibility to them. Below are examples of how to write your intention:

- I intend to be physically fit (be able to run five miles without exhaustion) by March 2010.

- I intend to live in a house by the sea in San Diego by July 31, 2010.

- I intend to weigh 10 pounds less by December 1, 2010.

- I intend to volunteer for three months in South Africa beginning March 2010.

In writing your intention, be sure to give an exact indication or measurement of the intention, time frame, and result you wish to achieve for yourself. In doing so, you will know when you have arrived when you get there. This is also necessary so that others who can help you know where you are heading and can assist you through the twists and turns on the journey.

Being vague or using generalizations does not help you focus on what it is you want for yourself in living a life that you love. So be specific: I want to be, do, or have "X"' and within a certain time frame . . . by

"Y.'" Now, do not worry if you don't know whether you will actually arrive there by that time. You can review your timeline at intervals.

Remember, you cannot write a general statement like "be happy by the end of the year" because you need to be very clear about what it is that will make you happier. Review Chapter 3 (Define Who and Where You Want to Be) to identify and clarify the areas in your life that you want to concentrate on for your journey so you can create greater happiness for yourself and for others.

Identify Your Super Champions

We have discussed the importance of having lifelines for your intentions. Lifelines are committed listeners you have in your life such as friends, family members, and colleagues who are willing to be your sounding board and who can hold you to account on your actions to fulfill your stated intentions. Now we can identify what we call Super Champions—those people who are similar to lifelines, though likely ones you have yet to meet.

Super Champions are people you may have identified (or could identify) as people who can help you with your intentions in a very big way. If you are up to creating a big possibility for yourself, such as starting a new business, you may need a number of people to help you with this endeavor. You can imagine having a monthly meeting of advisors who are sitting around your own round table (even if this is your kitchen table). Imagine all the people who you think could make the biggest difference to the success of your new business. Now imagine they are sitting with you at your table responding to your questions, challenging your ideas (in a positive way), and guiding you with the next steps to take.

Allow yourself to imagine the people that you have heard of or that you may know of as people who have done something similar to what you are about to do now with your new business. Imagine inviting them to join you at your round table. These people may include financial wizards, marketing mentors, and sales champions. Let your imagination wander. Think through all the people who you may have heard about, and talk to your friends about who they have heard of or who they may even know. Think about what kind of people you need to help you to work out your plans, guide your thoughts, and make sure you take the appropriate action.

Draw a picture of your round table. Put seats around it with the names of the people you have thought up even if they are people you feel you may never actually get to meet. Place the names around your table. Now imagine yourself actually having those people sitting with you and what life would be like if you had them there. What questions would you ask them? What actions would you like them to take on your behalf? What are you requesting of them all? Allow yourself enough time with this. Stop yourself from saying, "Ah, that's silly—none of those people will come and sit at my table." Of course you may not get exactly those same people around your table, although you may find there are others within your reach who you can call upon as your Super Champions. Your friends and family might even be able to help you connect with them.

You will need to think through the plan of approaching your Super Champions to request their help. Once you start communicating with people about the type of Super Champions you want to connect with, you will be amazed how the ripple effect will cause someone to come up with a great idea or person to help you. You will need to be open to communicating as much as possible with as many people as possible about the people you want at your big round table. This is something that people are reluctant to actually do. This is why they get stuck, resulting in them not having enough people to assist them with getting to realize their possibilities. Reach out! You know you can. Be courageous and connect with anyone and everyone you know to help you find your Super Champions.

Summary

Your desires are not intentions unless you add actions to them. Declaring your intentions for the life you imagine will empower you to take the steps necessary and provide you with measurement tools to assess your progress. Most importantly, you will claim a new-found freedom within the core of your being, one that allows you to dream of all the possibilities.

Review Questions for Declare Your Intentions

1. What are my concerns in sharing my intention (such as the concern that people will see me as odd, in a dream world, or just not used to sharing my intentions with others)?

2. How will I approach my champions, advisors, friends, and family (call them, meet with them, write to them)?

3. What would I like to receive help on?

CHAPTER 10:

WRITE YOUR PLAN

A good plan today is better than a perfect plan tomorrow.

—Unkown

---

*L*et's start on your plan.

You may remember in the Introduction that we indicated you do not need to create the entire plan for your entire life on this day (or any symbolic day such as New Year's Eve). You only need to begin. Even if you choose only one area of focus that will help propel you toward a life you love, you are one step further in realizing it. The intention is that as you go through this process, it will become simpler and more fun! After all, you are designing your life.

If you want the life and lifestyle you imagine living, you need to get started. You need to check in with yourself and revisit the questions:

- Do you know what is available to you?

- Do you know how to get what you want?

- Do you realize how your thoughts change your life and how your actions will change it further?

- Do you know what "happy" is?

- Do you know you are the cause?

- Are you aware of the contribution you must be to the world?

- Are you ready to get on with it?

This is the sequence we will follow to create your plan:

- Identify your areas of focus
- Declare your intentions
- Identify your gaps
- Define your actions
- Obtain leverage on yourself
- Assess your progress
- Identify and contact your Super Champions

Identify Areas of Focus

We can indicate what we want to be, do, or achieve, but have we really qualified the importance of this in our lives? There are only so many categories of your life to consider, and they have been rehashed in numerous books. So, rather than having you come up with them on your own, we list them below.

Please turn to the progress plan in the workbook (page 182). Complete each section of the plan as we go through the process step by step. In the plan, circle from the list below the **top five areas that require your attention**.

Remember the Change Equation? $D > (V + K + C)$. The D stands for the dissatisfaction with what you have going on in your life. As you assess what areas require your attention, consider what you are most dissatisfied with in your life. For example:

I Am Here:
Current state:

- Emotional
- Health
- Finances
- Family
- Faith
- Fun
- Relationships
- Contribution
- Personal

- Community
- Education
- Vacation
- Relaxation
- Wealth
- Business
- Home
- Other _____

Declare Your Intentions

Next, you will list your areas of attention (those you circled) and write your **intention** beside it.

For example:

I Am Here: Current state	**Intention**
- Health	I will lose 20 pounds by Easter.
- Finances	I will triple my income by end of year.
- Family	I will visit my family four times per year.
- Vacation	I will take one vacation per quarter (to Honduras, Greece, Cabo San Lucas, and Hawaii).
- Business	I will sign on four new clients, one per quarter.

Notice that the intentions are specific and include a timeline for manifesting each. Refer to Chapter 9, Declare Your Intentions, for help.

COMPLETE THIS SECTION OF YOUR PLAN NOW.

Identify Your Gaps

Next, let's get some facts. How far between your current state and your desired state are you? Let's assess the gap. With all the imagined aspects for your future life, look at where you are now and then look at where you want to be. What is missing in the gap? Ask this question: What has prevented me from reaching my desired state to date? For example:

I am Here   **Intention**
Current state

HEALTH   I will lose 20 pounds by Easter.
Gap
I am not exercising.
I do not watch my nutrition.
I have no eating plan.

FINANCES   I will triple my income by end of year.
Gap
I don't have a business or moneymaker in mind.

FAMILY   I will visit my family four times per year.
Gap
I don't have a plan to make this happen.

VACATION   I will take one vacation per quarter (to Honduras, Greece, Cabo San Lucas, and Hawaii).
Gap
I need to save money.
I'd like a traveling partner.

BUSINESS   I will sign on four new clients, one per quarter.
Gap
I'm not clear on what business I'm in.
I don't have a marketing plan.

COMPLETE THIS SECTION OF YOUR PLAN NOW.

Define Your Actions

Okay, now you know what you don't have or what you need. Let's assess the actions necessary to manifest the intention. What do you need to put in motion? Who do you need to be (to make it happen)? What do you need to do (to get it)? What will it require (to fulfill it)? For example:

I Am Here	Intention
	Action
	Timeline
Current state	

HEALTH

Intention: I will lose 20 pounds by Easter.
Action: I will join a health club.
Timeline: Today!

Gap
I am not exercising.
I do not watch my nutrition.
I have no eating plan.

FINANCES

Intention: I will triple my income by end of year.
Action: I will research home-based businesses.
Timeline: By 1/30

Gap
I don't have a business or moneymaker in mind.

FAMILY

Intention: I will visit my family four times per year.
Action: I will call Mom and schedule dates.
Timeline: Now

Gap
I don't have a plan to make this happen.

VACATION

Intention: I will take one vacation per quarter (to Honduras, Greece, Cabo San Lucas, and Hawaii).
Action: I will call a travel agent.
Timeline: Jan/Apr/July/Oct

Gap
I need to save money.
I'd like a traveling partner.

BUSINESS

Intention: I will sign on four new clients, one per quarter.
Action: I will write my business description and join the Chamber of Commerce.
Timeline: By 2/15

Gap
I'm not clear on what business I'm in.
I don't have a marketing plan.

COMPLETE THIS SECTION OF YOUR PLAN NOW.

Obtain Leverage on Yourself

In order for you to really stay true to focusing on the areas you've defined as priority for you, you must become crystal clear on why these are important to you. For example, if you chose health, you must consider and document what you will receive and what you will surrender as it pertains to living a life you love.

As you recall in the Change Equation, the C stands for the costs, or the consequences, of the change. Consider the costs and consequences of NOT taking the actions you've outlined. These costs and consequences will help you realize how much you value creating this particular change in your life. For example:

> If I accomplish my intentions for health, I will *receive*: Confidence in my appearance; energy to travel and be with friends and family; the interest in leaving the house; longevity; reduced risk of cancer

> If I do not accomplish my intentions for health, I will *surrender*: My ability to play with my kids; feeling comfortable in airplane seats and on long trips; the enjoyment of clothes shopping; staying off expensive medications

Consider asking someone to help you become clearer on and what you receive or surrender. Discuss with them why certain criteria make you happier.

Find pictures or symbols of the type of things you are imagining for yourself and keep them in your planner, on your mirror, or on your nightstand, wherever they will become a point of reference and reminder for you.

COMPLETE THIS SECTION OF YOUR PLAN NOW.

Assess Your Progress

You must assess your progress and determine where you are doing well—and where you need to take additional action—on an ongoing basis. Document your progress toward each intention, and be honest. Make course corrections as needed, and reach out to your lifelines to box yourself in so you will have leverage to box yourself out.

How often should you assess your progress? Add time to review your plan on a regular basis to your calendar/scheduler. We recommend at least weekly. It is useful to revisit your intentions on a daily basis and keep them centered in your mind and subconscious.

An example of recording progress and identifying course corrections follows:

I Am Here	Intention Action Timeline
Current state	

HEALTH

Intention: I will lose 20 pounds by Easter.
Action: I will join a health club.
Timeline: Today!

Gap
I am not exercising.
I do not watch my nutrition.
I have no eating plan.

Health Progress Report
I lost 3 pounds this week and must lose two per week to reach my Easter goal.
I am working out at the health club three days per week.
I found a workout buddy to motivate me.

I must:
Continue on plan!

FINANCES

Intention: I will triple my income by end of year.
Action: I will research home-based businesses.
Timeline: By 1/30

Gap
I don't have a business or moneymaker in mind.

Finances Progress Report
I have requested information on three companies.

I must:
Identify a financial advisor or business coach to help me. I will do this by April 1.

FAMILY

Intention: I will visit my family four times per year.
Action: I will call Mom and schedule dates.
Timeline: Now

Gap
I don't have a plan to make this happen.

Family Progress Report
I have two dates scheduled—March 1, June 10

I must:
Work with the financial advisor to devise a savings plan for the travel.

VACATION	**Intention:** I will take one vacation per quarter (to Honduras, Greece, Cabo San Lucas, and Hawaii).
	Action: I will call a travel agent.
	Timeline: Jan/Apr/July/Oct

Gap

I need to save money.

I'd like a traveling partner.

Vacation Progress Report

I researched prices for destinations.

I spoke with two friends who are committed to going on a trip, one in the first quarter, and one in the second.

I must:

Schedule the two trips for the remaining quarters, and identify traveling companions or decide to go alone.

BUSINESS	**Intention:** I will sign on four new clients, one per quarter.
	Action: I will write my business description and join the Chamber of Commerce.
	Timeline: By 2/15

Gap

I don't know what business I am in.

I don't have a marketing plan.

Business Progress Report

I wrote my business description.

I called people on the Chamber list to discuss their needs, and generated two requests for proposal.

I must:

Land my first new contract within the next two weeks.

COMPLETE THIS SECTION OF YOUR PLAN NOW.

Identify and Contact Your Super Champions

Think about what it is you intend for yourself. Who can help you? Who has the resources and the information that could be useful to you? Make a list of your top five or six Super Champions who you are going to declare your imagined future with.

My Super Champions are:	This person will help me with:
1. Becky	Losing my weight by Easter
2.	
3.	
4.	
5.	
6.	

COMPLETE THIS SECTION OF YOUR PLAN NOW.

Your Plan

You have just crafted the start of your plan for imagining being in a life you love. You may still get confused if you do not know how to lose 20 pounds, find a partner, sort out finances, and change jobs. Ask for help. Once someone has helped you with the many different ways you can approach your intention, you will begin to see the step-by-step, week-by-week, month-by-month progress you can expect to make, and you will ultimately see a timeline for the achievement of your intentions.

If you don't know what to do, just be silent and listen. Settling your mind and being in stillness can generate new ideas and better perspective.

The real effort when it comes to your plan is in managing your psychology around it. It means you must have a powerful belief system regarding what is possible for you. And, it means that you must be ready and willing to imagine being the opportunity in your life.

Imagine . . . if you realized all of your intentions.

What will your world look like one year from today?

_____

_____

_____

_____

Our primary intention for you is to follow through on the goal of living a life created and crafted by you, and inspired by good people and God (or creator).

Chart your roadmap . . . and start learning from your travels.

Now having intentions is easy, but fulfilling them, not so much. In the next section, we will discuss how to get leverage on yourself and how to manage setbacks.

Summary

If you really want the life and lifestyle that you have always imagined, then you must begin it—today! You do not need to have the entire plan for your life. Simply start the process by identifying areas of focus that can help you with your ultimate goal: a happier life.

Remember to declare your intentions, identify your gaps, define your actions, obtain leverage on yourself, assess your progress on a regular basis, and engage your Super Champions to help you.

Review Questions for Write Your Plan

1. What can I do each day to re-dedicate my commitment to my plan?

2. How often will I revisit my plan and progress to identify the next steps I must take?

3. Who will I share my plan with, and what will I request of them in helping to box me in to ensure I proceed with my intentions and plan?

CHAPTER 11:

PLAY YOUR CHOICE CARDS

It has been my philosophy of life that difficulties vanish when faced boldly.

—Isaac Asimov

You have now crafted your plan and will begin making progress toward the life you imagine living. Let's explore what can happen.

Once you have your list of your intentions and your action steps, you may get really confronted, or at least confused, about what to do next. You may also get overwhelmed, which we call in a very loving way the "Gotta Be Joking Syndrome."

When you declare your intentions and create your plan, do not expect it to be completed by the next weekend. It takes a while, and it takes concerted effort. Companies invest thousands of dollars in creating their strategic plans, and they often sit on a shelf unused and therefore valueless. You will need to invest many hours in the realization of your plan, and there will be times when you would rather not. When you make your excuses or choose not to manage the setbacks—and, if you get stuck there—your plan will be valueless, too. After all of your personal investment in getting to this place, ensure that your plan is not shelved but rather alive and a part of your activities and extension of yourself every day.

Let's now assess the "ah buts" that can get in the way, and acknowledge the choice cards you can put into play.

Rejecting the "Ah Buts"

As soon as you start defining your life the way you imagine it to be and the efforts it will take—even before you put pen to paper—what may arise are the "ah buts." They will arrive within seconds if they are in the possibility. They are natural. Some that will creep up on you or smack you in the face are:

- Ah but . . . I don't have time.
- Ah but . . . I don't know how.
- Ah but . . . I don't deserve that.
- Ah but . . . I can't.

Our view of ah buts is this: They are not, repeat **not**, reasons, explanations, or excuses. The ah buts are you saying to yourself that there are things to be handled, things to pay attention to if you stay with your intention to fulfill on the life you are designing. Framed properly, they can be a failure avoidance mechanism.

Not handled properly, however, and they will let you off the hook of taking power over your own life, serving as roadblocks in crossing your valley. If not kicked to the curb, they will enable you to stay within your existing life and comfort zone and not face the path ahead. Your ah buts have a bit to do with your belief system about your capabilities and what you deserve in the world. We will address your belief system in Part 3. For now, we realize that as you declare your intentions, the ah buts will begin to creep in. Note them.

What are your ah buts? What do you feel might stand in the way or be stops to you achieving your intentions?

In summary, everyone struggles at first with getting clear about what they want, working out how to get it, and then taking actions and making sure that they stick to the plan. It is called human nature, and you are human. As human beings, we fall off our daily commitments and actions at times, so you need to create a structure to get you back on. And back on. And back on.

Getting back on plan is a matter of first knowing when you've fallen off it. Add check-in points on your calendar. Schedule the time to assess how you are doing and where you need to redirect. You will need to choose to not play the hand you are dealt, but deal the hand you wish to play. This comes with your choice cards.

Play Your Choice Cards

Your life will include a myriad of choices to make over your lifetime. You will need to play your choice cards and realize that in the act of simply choosing, you are declaring a preference for yourself. Thus, your choices cannot be left to chance. There is power in decision. Real power. Your choices are limitless—infinite—and depending on how you look at it, that can be good or it can be bad. You are a product of your choices. Please, if you remember nothing else, remember to choose well. And when you don't, because there will be times when you won't, learn from it. Whatever choice you make, it is part of the larger plan for your life. Trust us. You'll land on your feet every time (with the right choices and even the not-so-right).

People make major changes in their lives based on either inspiration or desperation. Typically, it is the latter. Desperation is an enormous motivator. However, most often life runs along status quo—not too bad, not too good—and thus, that's how we live, status quo. There are a few things that are available en masse in life, and one is your Choice Cards. Once you play one, you immediately get another.

- You can choose to feel good or feel bad.

- You can choose to laugh or cry.

- You can choose to move or stay.

- You can choose to exercise or not.

- You can choose.

There are several ways to live your life. We likely live by the first approach:

1. **Ready, Fire, Aim.** We *choose* to pull the trigger and figure it out. We have learned to trust ourselves enough to know whatever happens, we will be okay.

Then there are others who live their lives like this:

2. **Ready, Aim, Aim, Aim, Aim.** They *choose* to not actually act.

And finally, there are others who live their lives like this:

3. **Ready, Aim, Aim, Aim, Fire.** Before they act, they *choose* to process information thoroughly.

For No. 2, this is the middle ground, and with no action, the result is no result. No choice. Eliminate that one from your repertoire, and go with either 1 or 3, depending on your personal preferences. Both work.

When you make a choice, just simply ask, "How is that working for me? Is it furthering me on my path to a life I love?" That's your anchor. Weigh your choices against it.

Some people may experience a lack of purpose in their lives. This has much to do with not being clear or authentic about what you really want in your life. Purpose will be missing if you cannot see what contribution you are making to people and to yourself. A sense of purpose flows from being purposeful, which is a result of designing a life you love.

To feel a sense of purpose, you need to be purposeful. You have to choose where you want to be a contribution to yourself and to others. You need to seek and get clear about what makes you feel fulfilled.

Summary

It is human nature to be scared about making change. Once you write your plan and see just what obstacles you have to overcome to transform your life, you may be hit by the ah buts. Don't let these get the best of you. Acknowledge them for what they are—excuses that can be dismissed if you are truly committed to your plan.

You have the choice to act or not act. In everything you do, there is a choice card waiting to be played. Use them wisely, but also remember that in taking a chance, you will more than likely land on your feet.

Review Questions for Play Your Choice Cards

1. What are my stops that prevent me from going toward what I want?

2. What are my ideas for handling the stops?

3. Who can help me?

4. What will I choose in order to make my life purposeful?

5. What will I choose to make me light up?

PART THREE:

IMAGINE BEING THE REASON

Man has been endowed with reason,
with the power to create,
so that he can add to what he's been given.
Anton Chekov

The heart has its reasons which reason knows not of.
Blaise Pascal

There is something in every one of you that waits and listens for the
sound of the genuine in you. It is the only true guide you will ever have.
And if you cannot hear it, you will all of your life spend your days on the
ends of strings that somebody else pulls.
Howard Thurman

In this section, you will learn to:

- Address the PINGs in life
- Develop your unshakable belief system
- Master the setbacks
- Take SPDs
- Make course corrections

CHAPTER 12:

OUR REASONS

B y now, you should be clearer on who you are and where you imagine being in your life. It is not a simple job to get to this point. Becoming clear on your intentions takes focus and conscious consideration. But once you do it, you'll be well on your way to living a life you love.

Often, our intentions are pushed along by certain drivers—they may come in the form of people, experiences, and life events. These drivers can be the reason for change, inspiring us to become who we will be in the world.

They may also be the result of difficulty or heartbreak. We call these types of drivers the PINGs in life. Even after you have clarity regarding who you are and where you imagine being, you will be the recipient of PINGs that can result in setbacks along the way, pushing you away from your desired goals.

There are reasons why we do and don't do things, why we move forward with our lives and why we give ourselves excuses to stop. There are reasons regarding where we are (or are not) today. You will need the personal power and the willpower to master and overcome the PINGs in life. In doing so, you just might be the reason others are inspired.

Kristin's Story

I've had a lot of PINGs in my life. Yet, I wouldn't change a thing. It is my belief that with the bad stuff handed to us in life, we receive an element of depth and understanding that we otherwise would not have awakened to. There is good that comes from the PINGs.

My mom was diagnosed with breast cancer. She is my rock, and the thought of losing her was devastating. Not knowing exactly how bad the cancer was and how she would react to treatment was brutal. She had a mastectomy, and we were ecstatic to learn that the cancer had not spread to her lymph nodes. She required no chemotherapy or radiation treatments. It was a horrible experience watching her go through this, but the whole process made us grow even closer and appreciate time together all the more.

Like everyone else, I've had to face the loss of family members. My stepfather's death was a time of great sadness and fear. My mom had to learn how to live by herself for the first time in her life. Russ was the love of her life, and she'd already lost so much. I missed him so much myself, yet I learned from this loss what love truly is.

My brother Kent's death was particularly hard on me. Yet in the midst of this sadness for my family, I witnessed what at the time seemed like a minor miracle—a hug between my mom and dad, and my father and his mother speaking for the first time in years.

The loss of my dog C.O. was another PING, along with the earlier death of his brother, Sarge. C.O.'s death meant the loss of my constant companion, the one who was with me through all the tough times. My ex-husband and I bought C.O. when we married, and I kept him after the divorce. C.O. brought me to my knees every night; I would lift him onto my bed and we'd play. He taught me to pay attention to how I utilize my time and with whom. I have only one "I wish I would have" that is significant for me, and that is I wish I would have worked less while he was alive and been present with him more. My life had a huge gap in it, and I miss him to this day. Yet with C.O. gone, I was able to travel more, and eventually I made the choice to move to the West Coast for another fresh beginning.

Lately, I have had some PINGs on the health front. I injured my knee returning from a business trip. An MRI revealed that I'd severed my ACL, torn my meniscus, and suffered a bone contusion and fracture. I did not select surgery, and through massive hard work I have been able to rehabilitate my knee with the help of some great physical therapists.

I think every time I've moved has been a PING of sorts. Interestingly, many of my milestones involve a move to a new location. Perhaps this is my "fresh start" or "challenge me" perspective. Perhaps it is a bit of running away, too. Moving is a PING because it involves leaving behind people that I love, though true friendships travel with you across time and space. And what I have learned through this process is that your stuff comes with you, so it is important to address whatever it is that has been your baggage or history that holds you back. Geography is not a cure. You will still have your memories, your emotions, your feelings, and yourself to deal with.

During my recovery from my knee injury, I realized that I was grossly unhappy—and lonely. I never admit that I'm lonely. I like to believe it is a state of mind, and I think often it is. You can self-talk your way out of being lonely, or take an action so you are not alone. I realized I was doing work that held little self-expression for me. I am the person who loves to dream, to dare to do what people think cannot be done, and I suddenly realized that I hadn't done that for months. I was living in fear of not delivering on expectations, and I was exhausted from swimming upstream and being tremendously off purpose. I was having thoughts of being the fat girl from the sticks instead of the audacious businesswoman who could make anything happen. My belief system had gone south and with it my confidence, my desire to jump out of bed and get going with the day, and my zest for living. I had to create change. I had to be the reason for that change.

Jaqui's Story

When I was two years old, I had a major PING! I was in an accident, and my left eye became lazy and turned inward as a result of the shock. I remember as a child being bullied and laughed at until the age of thirteen. I was called "specky four-eyes" and "Clarence the cross-eyed lion." I was constantly aware of my appearance and was very sad most of the time because I was not very pretty. I managed to throw several pairs of spectacles and most of my childhood photos down the household drain. At age eight, I received another PING! A teacher told me that I had to study hard in order to take care of myself because I was unlikely to get married (due to squinting). I did study harder, and that, in part, was a contributing factor to my success today. The PING helped me to study!

At age thirteen I had my lazy eye straightened. The ugly duckling turned into a pretty young swan. I was elated. I chose a new school to attend—two bus rides away from my former school so I didn't have to face any of those cruel kids who had called me horrid names for eight years.

I chose to go to university when I was eighteen and was excited about the adventure. Unfortunately, I received another PING at college. I got involved with a guy and got into debt bailing him out. I found myself going to the bank for a student overdraft. I was terrified. The assistant bank manager was concerned because I looked so pale. He enquired whether I was sick, and I replied by saying I was just very nervous asking for a £200 loan, at which he laughed and told me that if it were not for people like me taking out loans, he would not have a job.

As this crisis was going on with my finances, I also became more asthmatic—another PING! I found myself having to take better care of myself. I believe the pressure of exams and moving away from home contributed greatly to my health issues.

Another PING came at age twenty-nine, when my father passed away. He had been in and out of hospitals for years. I was suddenly called upon to care for my mum. Many years later she was diagnosed with terminal cancer, and during 2004 she came to live with my husband and I in our home. During this time, I did not know what to do for the best—take a year off work and be with her 24/7 or work just some of the time. I had to keep the business going to return to it after this period. Mum was great about this: She said that I should go to work some of the time so that we had plenty to talk about when I was with her. I managed to work and look after her along with many other people taking care of her, too. Instead of this experience being very disempowering, it was a very special period, and we had lots of time together while I managed to keep the business going.

My health took a turn for the worse at age forty-seven. The doctors did not diagnose the problem, nor did they seem to care, even calling me the "worried well." In January 2008, I actually felt like there was no point to living; it was the lowest I had felt in my entire life. I was fifty pounds overweight and thought that perhaps if I lost some weight I would feel a whole lot better. The clinic took blood tests to check for diabetes, and the results showed that I had an underactive thyroid. I was concerned and elated at the same time. Perhaps now I would feel better, I thought. I actually did lose forty-two pounds, and the new medication helped me begin to feel like my old self once again. My health continues to be an ongoing PING, so I am required to have more self-awareness about what I can manage and what I need to leave for later or for someone else. I listen to that inner voice, living each day by taking care of what I truly need versus being the can-do girl that can do anything, anytime.

Once we have our minds focused on our declared intentions, and we are clear on the choices we have made that we believe will lead us to a much happier life, we can then get on with the actions that will get us to where we need to be. Right? Not always so. Even with the best of intentions, we sometimes, and often, get PINGed—ping, ping, ping. Something can zap us or stop us.

Summary

At some point on your journey to a life you have imagined, you will have to face the unexpected. You will have to face the PINGs, those thoughts or events that can either empower and inspire you or stop you dead in your tracks. The determining factor in whether a PING is a positive or a negative driving force is you.

You are, after all, the reason for what happens in your life. How you react to a PING is ultimately up to you. However, remember this: You already know that you are the cause and the opportunity in your life. When you know who you are and have a plan for who you want to be, you have the reason for overcoming anything thrown your way.

You have the power over PINGs. You have the ability to face them, refocus your attention or change your view, if need be, and then move on. Do not let them compromise you, your dreams, and your desire to live a life on purpose and with purpose.

✦ CHAPTER 13:

MANAGE LIFE'S PINGS

Our greatest glory is not in never falling, but in rising every time we fall.

—Confucius

---

*H*ave you ever watched a movie that left you with a sense of empowerment as you walked out of the theater? One that had you cheering the protagonist for beating seemingly impossible odds?

Most likely you have. Over the years, Hollywood has delivered several powerful, true-life stories, including:

Rudy, in which Daniel "Rudy" Ruettiger overcomes physical and academic limitations in order to realize his dream of playing football for Notre Dame;

The Miracle Worker, in which devoted teacher Annie Sullivan fights through barriers to reach the deaf and blind Helen Keller;

Apollo 13, in which Commander Jim Lovell and his fellow astronauts persevere through a series of seemingly disastrous accidents to get back home;

Mrs. Henderson Presents, in which Laura Henderson defiantly keeps the Windmill Theatre open for soldiers during the bombing of London;

Braveheart, in which William Wallace stares down overwhelming forces and leads the Scots in battle to gain freedom from English rule.

Moving. Inspiring. Empowering. These movies resonate with us because we like to see people triumph. We truly want others to beat the odds, whether it is in love, sports, business, war, or life in general. We want happy endings.

Of course, on the road from youth to adulthood, we learn that not everything ends happily ever after. We come to realize that while we can overcome the dragons, poisoned apples, magic potions, and evil stepmothers . . . we still may not end up with the prince or princess. Life teaches us that.

But what life does not teach us are the skills to deal with the set-backs we may face in life. During our formative years, we are schooled on subjects that enhance our reading, writing, and 'rithmetic skills, but we are not taught the personal or life skills that we will need to effectively deal with the setbacks that do come along.

So why did you feel good when walking out of the theater after a movie like *Rudy*? Probably because you know that life is not always smooth sailing. It seldom goes like this:

It usually goes more like this:

Life will never be smooth sailing because there will always exist the crests (highs) and the troughs (lows)—and those troughs are the PINGs. Where you are in your life right now can probably be charted by the many PINGs you have experienced along the way.

Life really comes down to choosing whether you will let the PINGs rule you. It is within your power to take control of your life and take responsibility for your actions—just as Ruettiger, Sullivan, Lovell, and the others mentioned above did. You can develop the reasons, explanations, and excuses to *be* your best intention.

You *can* control the PINGs, to an extent. Yes, let us repeat that: You can control the PINGs . . . to an extent. The force with which those waves in life hit can take you by surprise. What's important is how you react to those waves—if you let them knock you off course, if you let them drown you, or if you let them raise you to ride new, unexpected crests.

Yes, the crests in life can be PINGs, too. It's all a matter of how you perceive them.

The Highs and Lows

PINGs are powerful forces. The analogy with the ocean is really quite appropriate because the PINGs that can affect your life come in as many shapes and forms as the waves upon the ocean. Some may be little ripples that are annoying enough to disrupt your plans, some may be high seas that force you to look for new routes, and some may be catastrophic, making you hang on for dear life.

You never know when the PINGs are going to hit, so you need to learn to recognize them so you can control just how much they will affect your life.

The Crests

These are what we refer to as the good PINGs. Have you ever had an occasion when an incident threw you off course and you cursed it . . . until you realized that, wait, there may be something good that can come of this.

Remember Jaqui's story about her teacher telling her she would have to study harder because she was not pretty enough to marry? Well, let's look at that. First, that teacher was just plain mean. What she did was PING an eight-year-old child for no reason. She put in Jaqui's head the notion that nobody would ever want to marry her. That's the negative PING. But there's something else that came of those teacher's words—a good PING: Jaqui did study harder because she thought she'd never marry. As a result, she did well in school, which set her on the career path she enjoys today.

There are plenty of examples of these PINGs in life—those seeming setbacks that ended up taking someone to new heights.

Oprah Winfrey was told by her TV station manager that she was not going to make it as a reporter . . . only to become the greatest female multimedia mogul in history.

Lance Armstrong was told that a cancerous tumor had metastasized to his brain and lungs . . . only to become the only cyclist in history to win seven consecutive Tour de France races.

Erin Brockovich was ridiculed by fellow employees for her lack of a formal law education . . . only to lead the largest direct class-action lawsuit in U.S. history.

What's important to remember is that PINGs—while they can be seemingly devastating at the time—can actually end up taking us to new heights. It's how PINGs are perceived that makes all the difference.

The Troughs

PINGs can get in the way of our progress toward our intentions. If not fully recognized and dealt with properly, they can stop us, knock us off the path, or cause us to be everything except what we imagine being. They allow us to talk ourselves into something or talk ourselves out of something. We come up with reasons, explanations, and excuses to *not be* our best intention.

Here are the four types of PINGs that can test your faith, will, and desire:

The Simple PINGs (simple, temporary). These have an immediate effect and are sorted out in a short time. Examples would be your car breaking down on the way to an important meeting or catching the flu when you are preparing for a big occasion. These are more annoyances than anything.

The Significant PINGs (significant, temporary). These have an immediate effect and may take longer to recover from. Examples include breaking a bone or losing a job. These are significant enough to cause distress, but do not typically last beyond a few months.

The Swift PINGs (simple, on-going). These are the simple things in life that suddenly pop into your brain and ultimately affect you over the course of your entire life. Examples include snacking on cookies when trying to diet or making the sudden decision to skip the workout for the day. These PINGs can be the most harmful because if they are repeated frequently, they can turn into recurring bad habits, affecting your mind and body.

The Sweeping PINGs (significant, on-going). These are the critical events that we carry with us over the course of a lifetime. Examples include the loss of a loved one, a divorce, or a medical condition. These PINGs can creep up on us when we least expect them. Even if you feel you have addressed the happening in your life, a new experience can trigger it and you may backtrack to the emotion and the concern you felt during the actual time of its occurrence. Typically, these PINGs teach us the most about ourselves. How we step up to manage these in our lives differs for each circumstance and can take some time to fully understand. The primary interest here is that you acknowledge that you are affected by the PING and that it is impacting how you show up in the world or whether you are moving toward your intentions. It may even require a course correction in your plan. That's okay. Just be sure that it is not given the power to interrupt the life you imagine for yourself.

There are many circumstances and conditions that can leave us cold. When PINGs hit, we can lose focus, motivation, and our reason for going on to a life we have imagined living. We can sense a loss of control, a loss of power, and, sometimes, a loss of will. The thing is, we are not our conditions and we are not our circumstances. These things are happening to us or around us, and we can keep our inner focus should we choose to—despite the conditions and the circumstances.

Power Over the PINGs

To gain power over the PINGs, we have to remain resilient. We may have to adjust to handle the situation and circumstances and review what we need to do next. If, however, we become reactive to the PING, then we will lose our power to focus and continue.

People will never blame you for being reactive; indeed, they may even allow you to use a Sweeping PING as the reason for why you didn't go forward with your imagined life. They might, but shouldn't you!

When the PINGs happen, use your lifelines. These are exactly the times when you need others to support you. It requires a lot of focus and a lot of courage to keep going when the PINGs are coming at you. You must gain power over the PINGs and victory over the setbacks.

Let's talk about power for a moment. *Power* is "the ability to act or produce an effect." It is the possession of control, and it is magnification, intensifying in scope or proportion. Your ability to overcome obstacles is directly related to the power of your imagination and the strength of your belief system. How you control your life in tense or stressful situations—and how you intensify that potential within you—will determine your success in handling setbacks.

Conversely, *powerlessness* comes from the feeling or belief that you have no control, no capacity to dig deep inside for that power to overcome setbacks. You feel weak and unable to cope. You cannot see the possibilities or believe in a positive outcome.

If you allow that feeling of powerlessness to master you, then you will be swallowed whole and spit out by life. If you relinquish your personal power, you will never be the person you imagined being.

And remember, there is no way to de-PING your life. There are ways to utilize the PINGs to your advantage or get past them when they stop you. It really is a matter of choosing whether you will let them rule you. Choice is focused effort. It is putting your attention on the happier self you want to be and not the self that you were yesterday. Today you will act as the happier self you want to be. After all, you really do get to choose—it is your life. You just have to do the work to be the person you want to be.

Summary

When you are faced with a PING, keep the following in mind: To get across the valley, to move from Point A to Point B, requires you to listen and to stay focused on your intentions. Address the PINGs in your life head on and see if they are providing you with the reasons, explanations, and excuses for not taking the actions needed for you to be in a life you love.

Review Questions for Manage Life's PINGs:

1. What have been my PINGs? Have some created unexpected opportunities?

2. What happens to me when I experience PINGs?

   ◆ Do I get overwhelmed?

   ◆ Do I hide out from everyone?

   ◆ Do I get angry?

   ◆ Do I eventually get inspired? How?

3. What do I need as a coping strategy for when the PINGs happen?

   ◆ What calms me down?

   ◆ Where and on what do I need to focus?

   ◆ Who do I need to talk to?

4. How will I ensure that my PINGs propel me forward in a life I love rather than stop me?

CHAPTER 14:

DEVELOP YOUR UNSHAKABLE BELIEF SYSTEM

Make the most of yourself, for that is all there is of you.
—Ralph Waldo Emerson

So we have established that life is not smooth sailing, and acknowledged and identified the PINGs in life. So how do we really get through all the ups and downs life throws at us?

Remember your core being? Earlier in the book, we discussed the notion that to achieve what we truly desire, we have to look inside at the core of our being and engage its spectacular dreams, its infinite possibilities, and its boundless energy.

That core—that strength inside you—has been developed from your belief system. Think of it as an internal navigation system that keeps you on course even when the worst of PINGs come at you.

If you have an unshakable belief system, you know without a doubt that what you set out to do or be is within your grasp to realize. Assess your belief system now by asking:

- Do I believe I can overcome any obstacle?

- Do I believe realizing my intention is possible? Do I believe I deserve it?

- Do I believe anything is possible?

- Do I believe others will help me?

- Do I believe in me?

Now, the stuff of life will get in the way, which is often a test of our ability to muster or rally our internal strength and belief in responding in a manner that creates a positive outcome. If you believe life should just be smooth sailing—a straight line from A to Z—then you are likely ignoring the factoring in of life itself, and the many variations in the situations, people, contexts, events, and daily living that will play into your every day.

These variables will affect your straight line, and life is full of variables. People vary in their behavior day to day, moment to moment. Customers vary in their behavior day to day, moment to moment. The weather can vary from day to day, moment to moment. The world of finance can vary day to day, moment to moment. Your health can also vary day to day and moment to moment. You get the point.

To believe—even for one second—that it is likely to be all smooth sailing is to fool yourself that getting what you want out of life should just come easy. That is not to say that it is likely to be hard or difficult. You just need to be open to the fluctuations that life is. What you thought would take only a, b, and c steps may actually take a, b, c, d, e, and f steps. Be open to the fact that it may take more than what you first planned.

As people, we can often default into thinking and believing that life should be easy as a, b, c or 1, 2, 3. Why is it that we think this way when we see thousands of people in the most extraordinary of circumstances—circumstances that are working against their best intentions—achieve their intentions usually because they have taken actions a, b, c, m, n, o, d, e, or 1, 2, 3, 10, 11, 59, 5, 8.

People get stopped when they allow difficult circumstances or the variations in life to stop them. They lack the belief that they are responsible for forward momentum, and for the actions and behaviors necessary to move on.

If you have difficulty truly believing that you are the master of your destiny, and that the power lies within you to imagine being in a life you love, we ask you to experiment with trying. You have nothing to lose and much to gain by telling yourself you can . . . and eventually internalizing this belief as part of how you operate in the world each day. An unshakable belief system has immense power in the process of manifesting possibility.

The XY Equation

None of us has the ability to control anything in life other than our own thoughts and actions. However, we are the constant that acts upon, and is acted upon, by various forces. How we react to those forces will determine the outcome of our lives.

Enter the XY Equation. No, we are not talking chromosomes here. We're not talking math or statistics either, although developing a belief system does include dependent, independent, and interdependent variables that you need to recognize if you are to take control of your life.

In this case, our equation looks like this:

$$X = \text{the variables in life}$$
$$Y = \text{you, the constant}$$

For example, you have a well-paying job that affords you the opportunity to live in a nice home and take wonderful vacations around the world. But then the recession (variable) hits and you are laid off. Now you are struggling to meet the mortgage, and the trip to Mexico has been cancelled.

What has changed? The economy, something you had no control over. But more importantly, what has remained the same? You. Yes, your finances have dwindled, and the finer things in life are put on hold, but you are the same person.

The question is: How will you deal with this change? Will you crumble under the weight of new challenges or will you rise up to face them?

Developing a strong belief system will allow you to deal with any crisis that comes along—and trust us, they will come along as surely as the waves upon the shore.

How do you do it? It goes back to that core. If you have a strong core, you will be able to cope with just about anything life throws at you.

You are the Y (and the "why") in every situation, and if you have a strong belief system, a strong core, you will be able to overcome any obstacle, any variable that comes into your life equation. Your belief system equips you with the creative ability to confront and deal with the problems that arise. It will arm you with the resourcefulness to face any situation—no matter how dire—and, if necessary, chart a new direction for the future. It will also inspire you. It will be the fire in your belly that will allow you to believe in the seemingly impossible. It will be the energy that will propel you through the fears and doubts.

Three Stories: Belief

Right now, we want to share with you the true-life stories of three incredible individuals who illustrate the power of an unshakable belief system. They each exhibit the strong core that we speak about, the one that allows them to deal with any crisis—and trust us, these three had their share of crises.

Subject 1: He was an activist who believed that his people were being oppressed, so he lent his strong voice to the growing numbers of those who opposed racial segregation. He was committed to non-violent resistance, yet was arrested for demonstrations and sentenced to prison. His belief system would help him endure decades of imprisonment.

Subject 2: He was an extremely intelligent man who believed that there was a better life than the one he had been living. He grew up in an abusive household and was eventually put in a foster home. As an adult, failed business ventures left him penniless and homeless. His belief system would help him avoid the alcoholism, domestic abuse, child abuse, illiteracy, fear, and powerlessness that had plagued his earlier years.

Subject 3: At the age of thirty-four, she found herself suddenly faced with a death sentence. Diagnosed with terminal breast cancer, she was told she had only months to live. Yet from deep within, she summoned up the courage to take on the cancer and live her life to the fullest right until the end, inspiring millions along the way. Her belief system would not allow her to relinquish her power.

In Chapter 16, we'll reveal how these three people used their belief systems to overcome the setbacks they faced in life. However, as you read on, keep these people in mind as we discuss mastering setbacks and making course corrections.

Summary

We don't have to tell you that life is not smooth sailing. You already know that. It does not come as easy as A, B, C. But we will tell you from our own experiences that it is a wonderful and enjoyable journey when you are open to and understand the fluctuations that come with it.

Be the constant. Believe that you are the cause, the opportunity, the reason, and the energy in your own life. Be the Y—and the "why"—at all times and you'll find that no X can stop you.

Review Questions for Develop Your Unshakable Belief System

1. How am I seeing my life—as the creator or victim of it?

2. What circumstances do I need to adjust from or adapt to for me to fulfill my intentions?

3. What are the barriers that I am seeing, and how can they be overcome in other ways?

CHAPTER 15:

MASTER THE SETBACKS

Anytime you suffer a setback or disappointment, put your head down and plow ahead.

—Les Brown

The truth is that life is full of setbacks and problems: There are changes in circumstances, people are inconsistent, the weather never stays the same, and finances flow this way and that. Some days we feel healthy, other days not so much. Life is FULL of setbacks, full of variations, full of inconsistencies and full of problems, issues, and uncertainty. We have not yet met with any person who is free of setbacks. (If you know of anyone who is, we would really like to meet with him or her!)

So now what?

If life is full of setbacks, problems, difficulties, and issues, should we just surrender at the start and say we have no control, no power over this or that? Let's not bother with the intentions we have to be the best of ourselves and be happier!

Again, you get to choose. You can surrender, as powerless in the matter of your life due to circumstances beyond your control, or you can choose to take it on no matter what (gets in your way).

So why not become a master of setbacks?

Gain mastery over the setbacks. Be their master rather than giving them power over you.

You would do well to take this on for yourself and for all others in your life to bring real power into your world and say "no" to being a victim of life's circumstances.

"I *can* handle anything. I *will* handle anything and everything that gets in my way of reaching my best intention." If you stand in a place where you say this, you will almost be there before you even know it.

Amanda's Story

Consider the story of Amanda.

Like everyone else, I've had my share of setbacks in life. I lost my dad when I was eight years old. When he died, it probably didn't devastate me at the time—as in a life interruption—but what I believed for the next thirty-two years was that everybody who loved me would leave me. So then I made that my self-fulfilling prophecy. Every time I got close to someone and they left me, I believed that part of it was that I had made it happen.

Dad dying did alter things: we didn't have anything. We didn't have a TV, and when we did get one, it wasn't colour. We had hand-me-down clothes and we had second-hand everything. Dad's death did impact me because I was always the poor one in the gang. Did that make me behave any different? Maybe it made me more determined to have things for myself as I got older, and to make sure my children never had hand-me-down anything.

The major setback in my life was dancing. When I was a little girl, I wanted to be a ballet dancer. I grew too tall, but I still went to a theatre school—that's what I did; I went to a theatre school to become a professional dancer and to get dancing qualifications. I was at school until I was eighteen years old. It was then that I had an accident where I smashed my leg up. When the consultant came to see me about three weeks after my operation and said I would never professionally dance again, I was devastated.

I always remember the consultant's words because I took him up on them: "My dear, find yourself a nice young man, get married, and have children." And that is basically what I did. I went home, started seeing my husband, and six months later we married. Just over a year after that I had my daughter, Vicky. So I did actually take him up on his words. Was that the right or wrong thing to do? I would never say it was the wrong thing to do because I have two beautiful children. Was it in haste? Probably. But I don't have regrets about being married.

I had a very strange marriage. My husband was in the army and away a lot. He had at least three affairs that I turned a blind eye to. Why? I was very, very happy. I wanted to be a housewife and a mother. I liked baking. I liked keeping house. I didn't want to have a career. I had no aspirations to be anything other than a housewife and mother . . . until he decided that he would have a relationship with the next-door neighbour, who was my friend. That gave me a really big jolt because it left me with a decision to make: do I sink or swim? In my mind, sinking meant having a council house, not having my own money, and having to go to the government for handouts. I decided to swim.

I started the swimming process in 1989: I picked my kids up and moved to Chesterfield, away from anyone I knew. This was totally out of character for me as I like to be around familiar people. It was a huge, huge step into the big world for me. Had that devastation not occurred, I might still have been happy being a housewife and mother. However, my life took a huge change in direction. I made my own future over the next eight years.

In Chesterfield, I was offered the chance to be a deputy manager in a retail store. Surprisingly, I found that I was really good at it. I was good at organising, motivating, and training people. I blossomed, and I went from strength to strength. In just eighteen months I had my first store; six months later, I opened my first green field site (my first site from scratch). I got involved with the town and became Chair of the Retail Committee with the Chamber of Commerce. I got engrossed in everything; I just wanted to learn. I was like a sponge, soaking everything up.

In late 1999, I was offered the opportunity to go into shopping centre management. I would say it was being in an open-minded place that led me to manage the prestigious Covent Garden in London. It's extraordinary to me how I had all this knowledge beforehand. I can sort of process it now that anything is possible. We've all got ability, but not many of us use it.

Things were going well until my mum's accident in 1999. It happened while I was flying in and out of America, doing a course in New York. I honestly believe that if I didn't have the knowledge that the course had given me to that point, I would have cracked, because life changed forever.

My mum—who had always supported me, always been fit and healthy, and is a wonderful woman that I most admire in the whole world . . . she is my inspiration—was suddenly devastated with the loss of her leg. Everything about life had to be rethought. That period of time when she first lost her leg was very difficult for everybody to get through. She had the whole "I don't want to be here, I'd rather not be here" attitude, and my brother just couldn't cope with it. My mum, who'd always looked after herself, had to now look to her daughter to help her get dressed and move around the house. It was a trying time for all of us, but really hard on her until she got used to managing things. Today, she is still an amazing woman to me, still an inspiration.

So my life has had its big changes, its setbacks. It is totally different than what I imagined it would be. I expected to be housewife and mother, and I never imagined anything different than that. I was never career-minded. It's totally different, but I wouldn't have it any other way, at all. And the nice thing is I can actually say I don't have any regrets. There are a few things I may have done wrong, and maybe I wish I hadn't done some things in the way I had, but I have no regrets.

I have to say that despite the setbacks, my life has turned out to be fabulous. Fabulous. It's great. Yes, I have changed direction several times. They were forced changes mostly—or maybe forced choices is probably the right phrase—however, through the work that I've done through Landmark and Deepak Chopra, I'm very chilled about interruptions now. Whereas for many years I thought myself to be a victim, I do not believe I am a victim anymore. I think setbacks are just disguised as opportunities, and I choose wisely.

Setbacks Test

Amanda is a good example of someone who did not let the setbacks gain mastery over her. Instead, as she said, she decided to swim, and in doing so carved out a successful career as a mother and businesswoman.

How do you typically handle the setbacks that arise in your life? Take a minute to answer the following question to determine if you are allowing setbacks to gain mastery over you.

How do you respond when something gets in your way of what you want to do?

A) Do you switch off and isolate yourself or take yourself away from the setback?

B) Do you stop what you said you wanted to do because of the setback (that is, what's the point of trying anyway)?

C) Do you feel a victim because of the setback? That life isn't going the way you wanted it to go, so you blame someone or something?

D) Do you moan and whine to many people about what is happening in your life and why you can't get on with what you said you wanted?

E) Do you get annoyed or even angry and take it out on someone, something, or yourself?

If your answer is A.

SYMPTOM: You end up procrastinating and putting off dealing with whatever the setback is.

SOLUTION: You need to confront it head on and work out the solution to overcome the setback. You may need assistance from others to overcome the setback.

If your answer is B.

SYMPTOM: You are giving yourself an excuse that it is too difficult or is not going to happen.

SOLUTION: Look at the reasons you are stating for giving up on your intention. Are the reasons real or are they an easy way out of having to handle the hard stuff when the going gets tough? Face up to the fact that all new intentions that require change to some degree are going to be uncomfortable. Talk it over with a friend. Share how you feel when you get stopped and what makes you want to give in. See if you can identify the trigger that has you give up on your intentions.

If your answer is C.

SYMPTOM: You talk to other people about why you cannot be or have your intention, and you say it is because of him, her, it, or them. You are avoiding actually talking to the person you are blaming.

SOLUTION: Your life may involve others who will have an impact on your intentions. However, they are not causing you to achieve your intentions or not. You will find people who are helpful and will contribute, and then you may come across people who just seem to get in the way of your intention. Face up to the people getting in your way. You may just be imagining that they are getting in your way. Have a conversation with them about helping you. If they do not want to help or are being obstructive, then review what other action you need to take.

If your answer is D.

SYMPTOM: You feel like you are constantly complaining. You get a bit of relief when you do complain and then, within seconds, you feel even worse then you did before. You start losing energy.

SOLUTION: Only complain to those who can do something to help you sort things out. Stop repeating yourself to lots of different people who cannot do anything to help other than listen to you. The chances are that they will get tired of hearing you go on and on about the same thing. Target the people who can help you move on and get through the setback.

If your answer is E.

SYMPTOM: Raising your voice, shouting, screaming. Being snappy with people. You lose concentration, you lose control of yourself, you lose your composure.

SOLUTION: Find something that you would normally find soothing, like a cup of tea, a walk around the garden or block, a walk with the dog, or taking deep breaths for a few minutes. Regain perspective on the situation. Put things into proportion. How big a deal can this really be? Is it life or death? Try improving your tolerance threshold or your patience. Take a step back and look at the situation from another angle or from another person's point of view.

Gain Control

So which one are you—A, B, C, D, or E?

Mastering setbacks requires your willingness to be flexible, to work with what comes up or does not come up . . . to work with what is getting in your way . . . to change actions when present ones are not making any difference to getting what you want and need. Mastering setbacks requires you to give up your dominance of the situation, that it should be a certain way, the way you thought it should be (easy, fun, straight-forward and quick).

Mastering setbacks requires your willingness to make it happen for yourself no matter what. Change, take another approach, create new opportunities, and talk to people to help you through it. Use your choice cards.

When things do not go the way we intended, we often get annoyed, frustrated, disappointed, upset, or even angry. Notice yourself being at the mercy of your *reactions* to what is not going your way.

Being annoyed, frustrated, disappointed, upset, or angry are not very useful emotions to hang on to; they evoke some of the most disgusting of behaviors in us. And yet, we allow ourselves to BE angry, upset, and annoyed, making it even worse for ourselves . . . becoming a victim, wallowing in our self-pity, blaming it, them, him or her. That is not helpful. We just get to hurt even more. Let us hurt ourselves even more than we already are. That really does not make any sense at all! Why not just beat yourself up even more?

Actually, don't beat yourself up. Here's a better idea: Take an SPD.

What is an SPD? It's a Special Person Day. It's our way of acknowledging that we are getting PINGed, allowing ourselves time to get angry or sad about it, and then moving on. That's the really important part to understand here—moving on. It's why we only give an SPD twenty-four hours. Any more than that and you will become one of those people who most likely gets on your nerves. You know the type: someone who mopes and moans about this and that going wrong—such as "my car won't start," "my life is terrible," "my kids don't obey me," or "I hate my job."

You know this person, don't you? Life's miseries, big and small, have become his or her mantra. This type of repetitive behavior is indicative of being stuck in the same place for much too long. It speaks of a lack of cause, a lack of opportunity, and, quite seriously, a lack of reason. Life will hand you setbacks. What you do with them will determine where you end up in life.

When you witness someone moping or moaning about PINGs, ask him or her this: "Are you having a Special Person Day?" It's a gentle way of asking if the setbacks are in control and sympathizing if they are, and then forcefully, and sometimes humorously, reminding the person that he or she is not the center of the universe—not the only person in the world to be experiencing what is happening at this given moment—and to get over it. You can also ask yourself and others, "How is that working for you?"

You are allowed an SPD every now and then, but do not let them become a habit. Acknowledge you are having a down time, but get right back up. Like Les Brown says, put your head down and plow ahead.

These variables in life, these setbacks, do exist and will continually challenge you. Having a strong core, a strong belief system, can help you overcome them and gain control over them. Use your imagination to get through the setbacks to where you need to be. Do not hand your power over to someone or something else. Do not wallow in the misfortunes. The minute you do, you lose.

Stay focused on your intentions, walking with the knowledge that you will handle any setbacks that come your way. Bring real power into your everyday life by refusing to be a victim of life's circumstances. If you can say, "I have the power to handle anything and everything that gets in my way of reaching my best intention," you will be one step closer to managing what PINGs you in life so you can begin living it in a way you love.

Summary

Mastering setbacks requires your willingness to be flexible, to work with what comes up or does not come up, and what is getting in your way. It requires you to change actions when existing actions are not allowing you to make the strides in life you desire. It requires you to entertain new options and not be tied to old ways of thinking.

Mastering setbacks also requires your willingness to make things happen for yourself. Be wise enough to welcome change, take another approach, create new opportunities, and talk to people who will help you through the problem.

Use your power to stay in control and evoke solutions that will serve you well in any situation, no matter how troubling.

Review Questions for Master the Setbacks

1. What is not going my way?

2. What is getting in my way?

3. What other ways can I get through this?

   • How will I take control of my life—or gain victory over the setback?

   • How do I reframe what I am saying to myself about what is happening or what has happened?

   • What new actions do I need to take to handle the setback and move forward with my imagined life?

CHAPTER 16:

MAKE COURSE CORRECTIONS

Once you realize how valuable you are and how much you have going for you, the smiles will return, the sun will break out, the music will play, and you will finally be able to move forward with the life that God intended for you.

—Og Mandino

You have a say in the direction you take and the choices you make, but there will always be the unexpected events that you will need to respond to when they happen. They may even require you to make course corrections.

Simply put, a course correction is a new course of action. You take a new path to or new direction to where you thought you wanted to be or would be.

Life's Twists and Turns

We'd all like to find our true loves and spend the rest of our lives with them. However, a cruel twist of fate can take our loved one from us. When that happens, we have to reset our intentions and redesign our imagined life. Even though we were not expecting to have to do this, we are forced to go ahead and do it. This is the way it is now, and we have to move on whether we like it or not. Often, the course correction gives us new opportunities that we may not have imagined if we had not had the experience of a setback. We may find a new purpose in our life and we may now move forward with that purpose, or we may meet someone new who will fill those remaining empty days.

Another example of a course correction has to do with a job loss. It is a frightening thing when one loses a job without much warning or notice. However, we can look at the future from where we are now and review where we wanted to be. Maybe our view has changed in light of new information. We can think about what we really have enjoyed in previous jobs and then go about finding a new job that is closer to our hearts. We may even find that a job that comes up turns out to be one of the best jobs we have ever had. New opportunities can come from setbacks if we look for new opportunities versus dwelling on our loss. Dwelling on our loss will not help us find new work. We can keep moving forward even though the recent experiences may have left us feeling a bit raw.

Of course, it may not be such a dramatic change in circumstances. There may be small changes that require us to adjust such as intending to run on a treadmill every day to get fitter and then having an accident and hurting your knee. Now you may have to go swimming for a while or do exercises from the chair so at least your upper body is getting a workout.

Think about times in your life when you intended for one thing to happen and then the circumstances stopped the intention from happening. Think about how you responded to the changes. Did you respond well and adapted easily or did you struggle to change direction?

Never think that making a change in any way lessens you or your ability to achieve your goals. History has shown that the greatest scientists, explorers, and businessmen have achieved greatness by recognizing that a shift in thinking or an adjustment to a plan has reaped far more benefits than originally anticipated. So don't be scared to reevaluate where you are and what you need to do differently in order to get to where you want to be. As the saying goes, change is good.

Andy's Story

Consider the story of Andy.

I always thought when I was a kid that I was going to be an architect. I used to love to build things. I played with all kinds of blocks and tiles. But I ended up studying not building or architecture, but actually stage design, painting, sculpture, and psychology. I met a woman who was an actress, a budding young actress named Barbara, and she induced me to take a course in the theatre department, which I did. I loved it and decided that I would get involved in stage design. She was going to be the actress, and I would design the sets; it was all going to be just perfect. Then life's interruptions got in the way.

Because I had a low number in the draft, I volunteered to become a helicopter pilot in the army. I was shot down three times in Vietnam. When I came back, I was kind of lost. I didn't know what to do with myself. I very briefly flew for NY Airways, which was like driving a taxi cab, and I hated it.

I got involved in a number of things, including the music industry. In the early '70s, I played and sang and was working at Geoff Hayes down in Greenwich Village. Bruce Henderson, a producer, was putting together a recording studio and invited me to stay for a few months to work with his other artists and cut a record. However, a big interruption happened: I wound up sleeping with his girlfriend, and he was very annoyed. I got blacklisted among pop producers—Phil Spectre and others in the Woodstock area—and I just gave it up.

Then I wound up deciding that if I couldn't do something that I wanted to do, maybe I could do something to make money. It seemed to be the thing to do. I had a number of friends who were making money hand over fist in the garment centre—it was the craze of the late '70s—and I went to work for a company. I learned the whys and wherefores of the garment centre, and made a lateral move to a company called Gala Creations, for which I worked fifteen years. I eventually became president of that company.

Then there was another interruption. I had a very serious back and neck injury. My wife, Miriam, and I had a very serious car accident very early on in our marriage, and I wound up having surgery for my back. I was unable to work for some time, so I wound up leaving that job and going out on my own, although I never made enough money to make it worthwhile.

There were so many changes in my career from then on. I wound up with an opportunity to work for a turnaround company called the Lawrie Corporation in Minneapolis—I still work in Minneapolis—and brought the family out there for a while. That was a huge change! My kids got an opportunity to train with one of the best coaches in the country, an ex-Olympic coach by the name of Eric Seiler. My oldest, Ali, met friends in the ski world that she is still friendly with today and became an expert technical slalom skier.

We moved to Connecticut and I worked in a partnership with a friend of mine doing coupons on the back of cash receipts. It was an idea whose time had not yet come. The companies that were advertising were not prepared for the volume of the response for the coupons. We did a thing for Kodak and it sold so many coupons—or rather it sold so much goods at a discounted price—that they dropped us because they said that there were too many coupons cashed. So I got out of that business—too soon because shortly thereafter the companies did figure out how to price and manage the coupons, and today it's a multibillion-dollar advertising business. We were one of the first to get in, but we were too soon.

After that, I met Tony Smith. I had known of him, but I was recommended for business by Dominick Valenti to meet with him and talk to him about possibly coaching my new business, which was called POS Abilities (Point of Sale Abilities). I met with Tony and was really interested, although my partner was not. I was not interested in coaching so much as in what Tony did. So I spoke to him the following week, and then I was working for him the following Monday. I did extraordinarily well until about 2002, when I was diagnosed with liver cancer.

From 2002 through 2009, there were four or five major situations associated with the liver cancer that put me out of the business for extended periods of time. And another car accident in August 2008 just about ended my life. I had broken my head in five places, my thoracic spine was fractured, all the ribs in my left side were either broken or cracked and penetrated my left lung, three of the ribs in my right side were cracked, and my ankle was smashed. It did not look like I was ever going to get out of that hospital. But I certainly did—and I was snowboarding with Tony on January 1.

Is my life what I imagined it would be? No. No, there were many points in my life when I did not think I would live too much longer, for a number of reasons, not the least of which is my partying days. They certainly took an impact on my health. But I had no idea that this is what my life would look like. It surprises me on a daily basis—sometimes good, sometimes not so good.

If anything else can be said to justify—to illuminate—my life that would be it has been an extraordinary rollercoaster ride. It's that line from Paul Simon, "Still crazy after all these years." The one thing that has turned out magnificently is my relationship with my family ongoing and growing love for my wife. So, that turned out even better than I had expected in my wildest imagination. It never even crossed my mind that I could love someone this much.

Have I put dreams on hold? Oh my god, yes. I no longer entertain most of them, although I still harbour the dream of becoming a musician—songwriter and singer. That one is still kind of alive, and I'm currently playing at least once a week with my friend. I haven't started writing again, but there's time for that.

Have I accomplished what I wanted in life? No. I have accomplished what I have accomplished, and I'm not unhappy with that. But I never expected to be sick at this point in my life. I never expected to be unable to be a contributing member of society. So many of the things that I would have liked to have accomplished, including financially, I did not. I like to think that I have an excuse, but I don't. I accomplished what I accomplished, and what

I didn't accomplish, I didn't because I didn't do the things I needed to do in order to accomplish them. It's not that complicated.

However, as for setbacks, I have a thing that I always used to say. I don't know, maybe it was my dad who taught me this: no matter what's going on, good news is just around the corner.

And as for things in life being easy, I remember the SEALS: the only easy day is yesterday.

Finding Your Purpose

As Andy's story demonstrates, life is a series of ups and downs, and many times we are forced to make course changes due to relationships, business, or health. And while some dreams for Andy have not been realized, what has brought him a sense of fulfillment is his relationship with his family, particularly his beloved wife, Miriam.

To lead a purposeful life you need the experience of being fulfilled. It may take some time for you to really look at your values and what makes you feel of contribution to yourself and to others. What we think makes us fulfilled may not be what actually does fulfill us. We need to take a good look.

Purpose is critical for imagining who you can be. Life is not meant to be lived alone, and the good that comes from our intentions is meant to be shared. When we can't see what the purpose of our being is, and how it might affect others, we become mired in self-doubt and find it harder to move forward.

As human beings, we fall off our daily commitments and actions and, therefore, need a structure, a purpose, to get back on. We need to remind ourselves that it is not only for us alone that we make the journey, but for others as well—our parents, our siblings, our spouses, our children, our friends, our co-workers, our church community, our world at large.

We need to believe that our intentions reach beyond what we hope to realize for ourselves. We need to imagine being the cause, the opportunity, the reason, the energy, and the light in our lives as well as others.

If the person you imagine being is not one who is making those contributions, stop and rethink where you are going. If you do not like what you see, change your course and set out on a new one that will allow you to live on purpose and with purpose.

Passive Hostility

You may find yourself feeling passively hostile to the situation you find yourself in when things do not go the way you want them to go.

There are those who choose not to stay the course and quit out of boredom and there are those who choose to stay the course because they are afraid of change. Either way, we can experience passive hostility. We bitch, moan, and whine about how our lives are not what we want, and yet we choose to do nothing about it. We can become hostile about it, although only in a passive way, speaking about it all the time while doing nothing about it. We become a broken record to ourselves, family, and friends who hear us day in and out.

Do you know of someone who just seems to be stuck in one place all the time and cannot find a way to shift gears and get on with life? You probably do. There are countless individuals who seem content with the lack of fulfillment in their lives, yet will be sure to remind you often enough how much they really hate it.

Perhaps it is due to a fear of what the future actually holds. We all have the capacity to influence our future, yet for many, the idea of what lies ahead seems too daunting a challenge, so they neatly tuck themselves into bed each night content that they have not fallen behind on expectations. Their frustration is a safeguard against any possible failings or shortcomings.

If you are one of these people, the first question you should be asking yourself is, "Why? Why do I feel life is so unfulfilling when there are so many incredible opportunities to be and to do?" Ask yourself what you are afraid of, and seek counseling if you cannot define what it is you want in life or obtain the commitment from friends to help you.

The second question you should ask yourself is, "How can I rekindle or re-establish my passion for life?" What will it take for you to access the true you?

Passive hostility can cripple you. It can rip your spirit from you and leave you powerless. You need to replace it with positive action. You need to find a purpose that excites you and makes you want to jump out of bed each morning.

Spend some time in reflection. Do a checklist of what you have in your life and what you want. Listen to your inner voice. If it's setbacks you fear, go back and read the section on how to master them. You have the power to create the life you want. Tap into your imagination and let the passive hostility go.

Three Stories: Course Corrections

The three people whose stories we shared in Chapter 14 are Nelson Mandela, Chris Gardner, and Jane Tomlinson. They are perfect examples of individuals who faced inconceivable setbacks and were forced to make life-changing course corrections that most of us can only imagine.

Subject 1: NELSON MANDELA

In the two decades that Mandela spent imprisoned on Robben Island, he imagined himself to be a free man. Not once during his twenty-seven years of confinement did it occur to him to believe he was anything else. He may have been locked away and sentenced to hard labor in the lime quarry, yet he imagined he was a free man. He continued to communicate with the outside world. He continued to be a voice of anti-apartheid. He continued to be a leader of the African National Congress.

Upon his release in 1990, Mandela went on to become the president of South Africa and a Nobel Peace Prize winner.

What, you might wonder, was the source of his strength? It was his belief—his insistence that he was a free man and a man who could change South Africa. While his captors might have thought they had him controlled, Nelson Mandela was, in fact, in control of his own life at all times. What life had thrown at him did not matter. Chains did not matter. His belief in himself and his determination to overcome the variables in life elevated him above those who sought to keep him down.

He remained constant, true to his convictions and his belief that one day apartheid would end and a new South Africa would emerge on the world stage. And it did.

Subject 2: CHRIS GARDNER

Chris Gardner is an example of someone who never gave up believing in himself.

The self-made millionaire entrepreneur—on whom the movie *The Pursuit of Happyness* is based—had a number of obstacles to overcome, and he persevered through the many setbacks in his life. His belief system told him that he was going to be a good father and he was going to succeed in the business world. And he did both.

Gardner believed that he was capable of creating a better life for himself and his son, and made the necessary course corrections to give himself the best possible chance of creating that life. With the help of a stockbroker named Bob Bridges, he took a training position at Dean Witter Reynolds. He studied and learned from those in the business, and eventually opened his own brokerage firm, Gardner Rich & Co., in 1987. Today, he is CEO of Chris Gardner International Holdings.

Gardner devotes much of his time to philanthropic work, working with and mentoring young people who need the same guidance he once sought, as well as creating low-income housing and employment opportunities in San Francisco, where he once lived on the streets. In addition, the multi-millionaire businessman has sought out new international ventures, including one with Nelson Mandela for emerging markets in South Africa.

Subject 3: JANE TOMLINSON

Jane Tomlinson captivated Great Britain and the United States during the last few years of her life. Even as breast cancer raged a battle inside her body, she never gave in, holding strong to her belief that she had the power over her life.

Millions of people watched Tomlinson, an amateur athlete, compete in marathons and triathlons during the last seven years of her life. When she died at age 43 on September 3, 2007, she had raised £1.85 million for various charities.

Many people who face terminal diseases are frozen in place, believing that life is over with the diagnosis. The major obstacle left cannot be overcome, and there is no need for course corrections as there is only one possible conclusion. Tomlinson did not ascribe to that line of thinking. In her mind, she was the cause of her reason, and that was to spread a message to people around the world.

What was the message that kept Tomlinson going through the pain? It was this: She wanted to share her belief that "there are lots of things that happen in life that you have no control over, and things you can do to keep control."

Jane Tomlinson had control over her life to the very end. She lived the life she imagined as a strong and courageous woman battling cancer—and ultimately won.

Summary

Life does not always work out smoothly. It is full of PINGs, uncertainties, complexities, and change. We live in a vibrant, ever-changing world that requires us to be tolerant and flexible, adaptable and agile. We have to bend and twist on the journey to deliver on our intentions. We may have to go round, over or through obstacles to get to where we need to be. It may not simply work out in a straight line from A to Z.

Part of the process in getting there is to have an unshakable belief system that can make things happen for you. While there may be uncertainty, your tenacity and perseverance will see you through all the twists and turns. Be aware that setbacks are just part of the process. It is almost inevitable that a setback or two will show up when you create something new, especially when that something requires real change in your behaviors, habits, and actions. Make a commitment to be more aware of yourself and what stops you in your tracks when you set out to achieve something. Make course corrections, if needed.

Review Questions for Make Course Corrections

1. What is not going the way I need it to go?

2. What other ways can I get to where I want to be?

3. What is it that makes this so challenging for me?

4. What am I constantly complaining about, but not taking the appropriate action to deal with it?

5. What will I do about it?

PART FOUR:
IMAGINE BEING THE ENERGY

Energy and persistence conquer all things.
Benjamin Franklin

In essence, everything is energy and cannot be destroyed.
Ted Andrews

In this section, you will learn to:

- ◆ Harness momentum
- ◆ Use your personal power
- ◆ Sustain and share your accomplishments

CHAPTER 17:

OUR ENERGY

*I*n this section, we will focus on being the energy of the life you
love—a life filled with passion and purpose while harnessing
momentum in your path on the way to attaining it. In essence, to this
point, you have already begun being the energy.

Our energy is connected to our personal power, the power we have
within ourselves to take the necessary actions to be in a life that we
love. Our personal power comes from being the cause of our lives,
creating and developing opportunities for what is important to us. Our
energy comes from facing up to, taking hold of, and overcoming the
setbacks that we experience. If you have read this book up to this page
and completed—or at least thought about your choices and actions—
you are on the path to creating and living a life you love.

Your energy for continuing is what will propel you forward to
realizing your intentions and attaining your goals. Your energy will
also attract others who bear witness to who you are and how you are
showing up in the world, and their support will help you sustain. As
you put one foot in front of the other, and take one action and then the
next, you will find yourself in a new place of expectation. You will have
achieved and now . . . you must celebrate.

Kristin's Story

It is December 31, a year after my originally declared intention
to write this book. I invested time on this day—as I've chosen now

to do every year—to review my year in the past and plan my year of the future. It's getting easier to do this. I understand the process and the flow. Today, I reviewed my goals from four years prior to date. I'm astounded at how many things I have accomplished—and that I didn't realize I actually had. In most cases, I did not accomplish my goals in the timeframe originally set. This is in large part due to the fact that I did not keep these goals and intentions front and center. Good intentions do not alone create a goal realized! It requires consistent focus and revisiting of our intentions to manifest them in our lives. Keep your plan—your intentions—front and center. Though I accomplished so many of my goals, I have now asked myself, "What if I had done so in the time I originally chose? What would my life be like if I had realized these sooner? How much more progress would I have made?"

I bore witness to Bishop T.D. Jakes preaching at the Potter House in Dallas, and his message was this: "Hold on one more day." He stormed and sweated from one end of the stage to the other as he wove a story of what his life is versus what it would have been had he not held on for one more day. Two hours of my life has never passed so quickly; I was hooked on his every word and action. Fascinated and bowled over by the knowledge that had he not held on, he would not be before me and the thousands of other people in attendance. He would not have just returned from Nigeria where he preached to 100,000 people. He would not be changing lives so distinctly every single day. So, hold on . . . who knows where your personal power may move you and others.

Knowing that I was off-balance in some areas of my life, I recently asked a friend for help. We were sitting at a Del Mar, California, restaurant by the ocean. I was feeling overwhelmed having just set my New Year goals and knowing that I was facing the busiest, most challenging year of my life from a business standpoint (and personal probably!) The sun was brilliant, surfers were catching waves, dogs were playing, and children were swimming. My friend and I were merely there to have lunch and enjoy, but I very consciously asked for her help with two items: 1) helping me choose to meet my life partner and to generate opportunities for showing up in places where he may also be; and 2) to help me by calling me out when I let work and making money get in the way of accepting invitations for fun and new experiences. Her response was to immediately accept my requests for help and even offer a few requests of her own. Now we are in it together. I know that when I see her, it will be on her mind—and mine—and we will discuss it. I'll have to own up to my progress, or my lack thereof. I need the pressure to become the gem or I could well remain a lump of coal for another year.

Jaqui's Story

This year has been a big year. As the year closes, I can say that many of my intentions have been realized, and some have not. It has been an incredible year of accomplishment. It has also been a difficult year of working and living with people who are facing the impact of the recession. In business, we have achieved another successful increase on the previous year inside of the global downturn. At the start of the year, I was frequently asked "how's business"? Most people expected me to respond with gloom and say "not so great." I took a view that this is probably one of those years when people might need me most to get through the hard times, and I framed my response accordingly. We have gained new clients that we are very excited about, and we are developing new partnerships with various people.

We have nearly completed the writing of this book. This has taken enormous focus and real intention. There were times during this year that the book could have come to a halt. We realized we needed help and we reached out to people to help us. The book is looking more useful than we had ever imagined as we receive early feedback from our friends. It has been a time of learning new skills, developing new opportunities, meeting new friends, and facing new challenges.

We now have the house in Mallorca that took a lot of working through and special requests of people. It is more beautiful than I imagined, and the location is perfect for our needs. It is a pretty spot near a natural harbor with some wonderful walks. The house is big enough to live in all year round should we choose that in the future, though small enough to manage and take care of.

My health has been better than the previous year, though the extra pounds started creeping back on in the summer months. I will get back on track with keeping the weight off and not be in a constant yo-yo with it. The eating plan is working well, and I see that I need to keep alcohol strictly to weekends and in moderation. Although we have had some great times this year with our family, I have not had enough time with my friends and family, and we are planning this in for our next year. We intend to be with our family in Mallorca during next year, and we look forward to organizing events with our friends. We realize that scheduling the occasions for special events will keep us focused to fulfill our intentions.

I truly believe that working through the process of creating and generating intentions makes it more likely for those intentions being realized. We get closer to living the life we imagine for ourselves, and we spend more time living a life we love than we would have without that same intention, commitment, attention, and action. I have been in this process every year for more than a decade, and I really cannot believe that I am living a life that I imagined back then. I do not have everything handled, and there have been some very unexpected interruptions and course corrections in my life. Yet even though there have been setbacks, disappointments, twists, and turns, I got to where I am today—which is a lot further than I imagined a decade ago.

Summary

Passion ignites energy and so does purpose. It is said doing what you love does not feel like work. What if being in a life you love filled you with energy? When you look back on your life one year from today, we want you to realize that how you decided to live every day made a difference in where you are. Will you be the energy fueling your future?

CHAPTER 18:

HARNESS THE MOMENTUM

The world is wide, and I will not waste my life in friction when it could be turned into momentum.

—Frances Willard

---

*T*he interesting part of realizing that you can imagine being in a life you love is that the imagining, and the effort, is a continuous process. The more attention you give to your intentions, the more progress you will make. Still, not all progress will happen overnight. Many intentions manifest themselves across time, as with weight loss or building a new home. Other intentions can be accessed immediately, as with choosing to be positive or giving your time to someone else. The energy you give to your intention of living a life you love will directly correlate to your results.

A fallacy regarding change is that it happens immediately or in massive quantities. Sometimes it does, though change mostly happens one small step at a time. The pace of change is, in part, dependent on you and in part dependent on the environment—that is, others and just basic elements of the change cycle. When you become clear on what you want to be and achieve in your life, it is easy to become impatient. Realize that lasting and significant change is often a lifelong journey. Maintain your focus, and attach your energy to the knowledge the outcomes will come.

You may notice that as you pay more attention to one intention, the others somewhat suffer or get left in the dust. This is normal. You will tend to focus on what is most important to you—or often what is easiest—in the moment. If you need to generate more income, you may work more and take care of your health less. If you want to be madly in love, you may invest more time on relationships and less on developing your business or studying for school. Your life is not a well-oiled machine. It has glitches and potholes. You will bounce through them, but the main thing is to be aware. Stay tuned in to your entire life, your whole plan, with all of its intentions. Give each a piece of your attention and energy. Realize that as you take action—big or small—you are a step closer to your result. Also realize that in inaction, you are reaping the consequences of more time passing you by without moving toward the life you love.

If you are choosing to live a life you love, are you completing your assignments and the thinking that is required to go into each step of the process? How are you feeling about it? Are you clearer or more confused? If you stop and start, stop and start, you will not reach your result quickly and may even bounce off the path. Just keep the wheels turning. Momentum is obtained and sustained with forward progress.

Michelangelo did not paint the Sistine Chapel in a day, but one brush stroke at a time. Rome wasn't built in a day. Colonel Sanders never gave up on his extra crispy or original recipes, pedaling his chicken door to door until he developed a global franchise (and he did this at retirement age). Mother Teresa and Gandhi did not earn their reputations by suggesting peace only once. They stood for it, across their lifetimes.

Mothers do not raise their kids within the first year of life, but rather support and teach them across time as they learn and grow. As a matter of fact, your plan for your life is much like the needs of a child. It requires you to nurture it, attend to it, and even play with it every single day. It requires you to be who you need to be to achieve the life you love, to act on those items that result in progress, and to realize that the time it takes is the time it takes . . . stay the course. Have some grit.

You may have discovered in the process of creating a life you love that you often receive more questions when you ask questions. This is normal, so do not be concerned. Certainly, do NOT stop or lose your energy. We are conditioned through the years to expect answers. Trust us when we say that the ability and the willingness to ask good questions is the best method for becoming clearer every day on what you want, why you want it, how you will get it, and by whose help. Write your questions as they arise, and discuss them with your lifelines and Super Champions. If you doubt yourself, speak up and also listen. You will be guided back to the path.

You are likely discovering more *ideas* than actual answers. The primary achievement for you is staying in motion. Keep asking and thinking and writing and you will stay in motion—you will achieve momentum. When you tune in to tuning up your life, you do instigate some chaos for yourself. This chaos creates energy, and it propels you to what's next.

Becky's Story

Consider the story of Becky.

I am the mom of two young children, a wife, a sister, a daughter, a college student and a daycare provider; I also sell jewelry and bake cakes to supplement my income. I am busy, and though I am often tired, at this point in my life I would not change how I use my time and energy every day. I decided to go to college in my thirties, and I have earned my associate's degree so far. I will not let anything get me off track in accomplishing my goal of receiving my bachelor's degree. I am motivated by my goals and my sense of accomplishment. If I start something, like getting my college degree, I plan to finish it. It is important to me because it relates to my daycare that I've operated for more than twenty years, the kids whose lives I impact, and my own kids. The better I am, the better I am for each of them.

I wish I would have changed how I used my time and energy ten years ago, although I wasn't ready at that time. Not having a college education was a point of insecurity for me. It made me feel less than what I could be. It took someone to believe in me, to give me a boost and encouragement that helped me to refocus and believe that I could go to college. At first it was incredibly difficult and I was unsure of myself. Now, even if I stay up past midnight to finish a paper or study, I don't get overwhelmed like I used to. I know that when I start my classes—or even a new business—it is going to be hard. I realize that it takes one step at a time, and I will get through it. I have more stamina, and that came with patience, practice, and persistence. The biggest change in me is that it takes me a couple of days or weeks to process it, but I work through it and get it done.

People often ask me how I manage it all and why I take on some extra things for other people. First, I manage it because I am a list-maker. I try to accomplish at least two items on my list every day. If I don't check them off, I don't beat myself up. I just get up in the morning and I don't give up until I get it done. As for the extras I do for people, like wrapping gifts, baking cupcakes, or organizing birthday parties, well, this just means a lot to me. I care about this, and investing my energy in doing these things for others actually does more for me. I also know it is meaningful to others. It's part of what makes me happy. I know I get over-extended and that I have made the decision to do so in some cases, but I would not change that. It means too much to me. Honestly, the way I get it all done is that I just don't stop. From the moment I awake, I am on the go. I don't sit down; I just keep going.

I don't always feel like I have the energy to get it all done. I've learned to prioritize things like vacuuming and dusting. I love to work out, and my health and fitness are important to me. My workouts have been suffering with balancing so many responsibilities. Sometimes this means I have to go for a run in the wee hours. If I had more energy, I would definitely get more workouts in, and I'd plan more activities with my kids. At times, though, things have to be put on the back burner, and I'm getting better about managing that. There are times when I just need to vent, and there are times when I will ask for help. I think that, as women, we have trouble asking for help. It makes us feel like less than we are, but we each have many people who will lend a hand if they know we need it. We do self-impose some of the busy-ness and sense of responsibility for our homes and kids. I think this is because of how many of us were raised. I think about my own mom, who has raised several children and is now contending with cancer. My wish for her is that she utilize her energy selfishly for once in her life, that she do something for herself that she enjoys and that she has never done.

As a young girl, the only thing I really imagined being was a mom, and now I am. I am most proud of my kids, and when they see me working hard to sell my jewelry or obtain my degree, they know they need to work hard to go to college and enjoy a good life. I want them to know that when they start something, it is important for them to finish. What I want for them is to be compassionate and to care for others. I want them to remember our laughter together. I want them to have everything I've had, and just a little bit more.

To maintain your energy and rejuvenate, my advice to others is to carve out some time for yourself wherever you can find it. Plan trips away from home where you can regroup, relax, and have fun, where no one wants or needs anything from you for a while. No matter what it takes to make this happen, know that it makes you a better person, a better wife, and a better friend.

I don't expect other people to do the things I do, although if they are unhappy in their lives, it does take concerted effort to improve and change. If someone is depressed, they should get in motion toward what they prefer to be or have. Talk with your friends or family, get feedback and validation, do your research, make some phone calls, make up your mind, and go for it. There is a lot of possibility in how we use our energy to help ourselves or others. People have to want it for themselves and for no one else. Once you decide on what you want, keep working at it and do not give up.

I am truly happy, and the energy I expend each day is fulfilling. Of course, I wouldn't mind just a little more time to relax! At the end of a day, and usually on a weekend—if I'm not up late to finish homework—I like to put my feet up and phone a friend to catch up or have a chat with my husband. Even though I am so busy, I would not change much in my life. In many ways, I'm living my dream.

Displaced Energy

What is the significance of Becky's story? Well, on the one hand, it's a perfect example of how keeping in motion can help you accomplish the goals you've set, whether they are long-term or short-term. In Becky's case, she knows that she is the cause, the opportunity, and the reason for the life she lives, and she is driven to accomplish the goals she sets.

There is an element of caution in Becky's story, too. We can often experience a disruptive force that often quietly and subtly creeps into our lives and obstructs the courses we have charted: we call it *displaced energy*.

Too often, we supplant the energy we have stored up for our dreams to the care of others. We devote so much time and energy to our family, friends, and associates that we have little left for ourselves. Granted, at times, this is unavoidable: As parents, we need to invest the required time to properly raising our children. However, all too often, others' needs come before our own.

Have you ever set aside a day for yourself and then shelved it because a friend needed your counseling? Have you ever thought to work on a project or hobby you love only to have a phone call asking you for a favor delay it? Have you ever wanted to work on a goal you have set only to have your spouse or significant other request you give him or her your attention?

At times, our hearts just cannot say no to the requests and sometimes, demands from others. We tend to put others first, and in doing so, fall off course. It is during such times that we need to focus on our energy and make sure that the momentum that is keeping us going is the momentum that will carry us to our intended dreams.

Do you remember that line we talked about in Life PINGs? Life is not always smooth sailing because it seldom goes from A to Z as planned. The PINGs can cause you to make course corrections, but so too can the energy you displace on the needs and dreams of others.

Now, we are certainly not saying that energy focused on others is wrong. What we are trying to get across to you is that you need to be aware of how you are using your energy—that you are allowing enough of it to focus on the intentions you have made.

To keep the momentum going for your dreams, be sure to allot the appropriate amount of time needed to keep on course. A life lived in service to others is wonderful, but a life—your life—void of the energy needed to stay the course you have set will keep you further away from the life you have always imagined living.

Tips for Harnessing Momentum

The key to harnessing momentum is simple—you must take action. And you must do so daily. Declaring an intention does not mean it will happen unless you do something about it. One way to keep your focus is to keep your plan in front of you.

Your plan contains the action steps and considerations for how you will go about achieving your intentions. It will remind you of where your energy needs to be directed. Place your plan in your wallet, on your mirror, in your car, in your planner, on your nightstand, or on your desk. Read it and revise it every day, if possible, and check in on what you are doing to accomplish your intentions. Your subconscious will also continue working for you. It will generate ideas or emotions that help you stay the course or jumpstart you when you might be flat-lining.

Another way to harness the momentum is to tune in to what or who you receive energy from. Think about what would make you want to jump out of bed each day because you are so jazzed about the possibilities associated with it. When you feel a lack of momentum, reach out to your lifelines and Super Champions and enlist them in your cause, opportunity, and reason. Seek their energy to fuel your own, and ensure you give them permission to hold you accountable. Consider taking a day to only do the things you love. Re-energize, and then return full force to the actions that will achieve results.

Use these checkpoints to assess your status:

- Where have you taken action and where have you not taken action?

- What do you need to do right now?

- What is stopping you? What will you do about it? Whose help do you need?

- Does each intention continue to be important to you? If so, what now? If not, what next?

You can also revisit the change equation—$D > (V + K + C)$—and ask yourself, "What are the costs and consequences of my not taking action?" If in a year from now you have not accomplished what you set out to do, how will you feel? What will your life be like? Who will you have let down? Kick your excuses to the curb and get on with it. And if you have not made as much progress as you would have liked by that time, then forgive yourself and get moving. There is no sense in beating yourself up. It is what it is. You are where you are. Determine what you can do right now to achieve momentum and do it.

Sometimes, when you need to re-energize or access your energy within, you may need to be in silence. Just breathe. Other times, you may need to make some noise. Play music, dance, sing at the top of your lungs, or make yourself (and someone else) laugh. Get your body and your mind in action.

There is no time like the present. Get started and keep moving, even if it is a measured step at a time. Stay in action to pick up the momentum. A friend of ours says (loudly!), "You do not have access to tomorrow! Who knows if it will come! What are you waiting for? Get moving NOW!" Seriously, instilled within us as humans is this mindset that we do have all the time in the world. We do not. Our life spans are finite. It's not something fun to think about, though we ask you to think about this:

At the end of your days, what will make you feel that your life is incomplete if you do not accomplish or realize it?

On the flip side, what will make you content that you have lived a life you love, that you can say to yourself, "Well done!"?

One of the most natural resources you have within your grasp is your energy. Maintaining it and applying it is crucial to your forward momentum.

Summary

To keep the energy in your life going, you must harness the momentum. You must keep in constant motion in thought and action. Do not be discouraged when the change you desire does not happen overnight. Change occurs step by step, thought by thought, and as long as you keep moving toward your goals, you will see the desired results.

Review Questions for Harness the Momentum

1. How can I create a more detailed plan of how to realize my intentions?

2. Are my actions consistent with my plan?

3. What adjustments do I need to make in my actions and activities?

4. What's my energy level? Where and how do I need to re-energize?

CHAPTER 19:

USE YOUR PERSONAL POWER

Personal power is the ability to take action.

—Anthony Robbins

*A*s is evident in this process, once you define what it is that you want it is then often a matter of staying the course. This requires the utilization of your personal power. Movement, action, and momentum require you to choose to access your personal power.

To us, your personal power is exercised through:

- You, being the **C**ause of designing your life.

- You, being the **O**pportunity maker in your life.

- You, being the **R**eason for momentum in your life.

- You, being the **E**nergy responsible for your life.

Accessing your personal power is first a matter of realizing that you have this power within you. Today's society tends to place responsibility outside of individuals—on government, parents, and employers—rather than making us realize that what we want in and out of life is fully a matter of us defining it and making it happen. Accessing your personal power can be as simple as this:

- I intend to do/be/feel/think X. (Define it.)

- I must manifest this by doing/being X, Y, Z. (Start it.)

- I must utilize the help of A, B, C. (Obtain it.)

- I must continue my focus and efforts while I realize my intention. (Sustain it.)

- I must revisit my intentions and reassess, refine, reframe, or redefine. (Evaluate and improve it.)

Accessing your personal power is a matter of conscious consideration and conscious action. Sustaining your personal power is a matter of commitment to consistency in your conscious consideration and conscious action. Many of us are gung-ho at the start, and then we have a pretty slow finish (or never finish). Sustaining your personal power is tough only from the standpoint that you decide (consciously or not) to use it. It is always within you. It is always available to you. You own the master set of keys and only you can unlock it. Re-read the section on mastering setbacks. It is the best way to kick your personal power into top gear and take responsibility for your own life.

Your personal power also includes accessing your unshakable belief system. When you believe that all is possible in your life, there is a subtle energy that is released within and around you that attracts the opportunities you wish to create.

When you need to energize your personal power, utilize the following IMAGINE BEING method:

I—Instigate change and create a challenge for yourself.

M—Move—take action!

A—Access your inner confidence and belief system.

G—Get over complaining.

I—Involve your lifelines.

N—Nurture your choices.

E—Embrace and develop a plan.

B—Be accountable.

E—Eliminate your setbacks.

I—Involve your Super Champions.

N—Navigate your course corrections.

G—Give and accept assistance.

Personal power is about accepting that to get what you want out of life, you have to take responsibility for making it happen:

- You need to choose what you want to create for yourself. This takes inner soul-searching and being honest with yourself and others about what makes you feel happy. Face up to the things and people who are not making you happy. Make choices that are consistent with your intentions for the life that you have imagined.

- You need to move and take the necessary actions. Without action there is no movement, no progression, no result. Actions are required to get you where you want to be. Some of the actions you will enjoy and embrace, and others you will not like as much but will have to do anyway.

- You need to believe in yourself. If you cannot believe in yourself, then how are you going to get to where you want to be? We all have inner voices that speak to us about not being good enough, worthy enough, deserving enough, or just plain *enough*. You have the choice to listen to those voices and give them power over you, or to ignore them when they come to you and gain power over them.

- You need to stop complaining and get on with what needs to be done. Complaints dilute your power. We all have complaints. We have to deal with all those things we are complaining about as soon as possible or just stop complaining about them. Really, what can we really do to change the weather in our hometown?

- You need to create your plan. Make sure that you plan your goals and develop a timeline for doing the activities that are required. Without the goals you will not be focused, and without a timeline you may not get things done by the time you need them done.

- You need to involve others in your plans. Attempting your intentions on your own is way more difficult than attempting them with the help of others. There are many people to help you. Allow yourself to be contributed to. Ask people if they can help. Accept that some will want to help and others may choose not to. Either way is okay. Just ask enough people so that you get some who agree to help you. Find your lifelines.

- You need to be accountable for all the things that need to happen as well as for all the things that did not happen when you wanted them to happen. If things are not going to plan, then review your plan and make changes to get yourself back on track.

- You need to manage your setbacks. There will be some problems, obstacles, issues, and difficulties on your journey to the life you have imagined for yourself. Hopefully, the setbacks will be small. Master the setbacks. Do not let the setbacks take control over your intentions and your plans. Look at the setbacks from various angles and assess what your next steps need to be in light of what has happened. You will find you can get over, around, or through any setback that gets in your way, providing you are willing to deal with it and not cave in to it.

- You need to identify your Super Champions, those people who are experts or masters at what you are about to do for yourself. Approach them, or people like them that you have identified, and request their help. If they decline, find others who can help through your network of friends, family, and contacts.

- You need to change course if new information comes along that impacts your initial intentions. It is acceptable to change course if you find yourself in a new situation that you had not expected. Review your choices. Make new choices.

- You need to give assistance to others who you can help and accept assistance from people who can assist you. Allow the contribution in. People enjoy being of contribution to one another. People like to feel they have made a difference in the life of another.

Human beings are professionals at being human. People are people. We set off, we continue with our goals, we get sidetracked, and we get focused again. Being human does include falling of the pathway of our intentions. The silver bullet is this: Be witness to it when it happens. Pick yourself up. Dust yourself off. Put one foot or thought in front of the other and continue again.

It is always easier to be lazy or put something off until tomorrow. Ask yourself what else you could be doing with your time. Are you telling yourself you deserve the downtime, or are you putting off today what could be a step in the direction of the life you love tomorrow? It's a matter of weighing what you get and give up if you do. Recall that the opportunity you cultivate happens in the moment of choice or the moment of inaction.

Stay the course! Hold on for one more day. Tune in to your personal power. When life gets off kilter, exercise your mental muscles to regain a foothold.

Summary

Personal power is conscious consideration and conscious action—that core belief within you that all things are possible. You are in control of how that power is wielded. You are responsible for whether it remains idling as your life passes by, or if it is shifted into high gear to open up the possibilities to you. Your personal power is within you. It is already available to you. You just need to access it. Use the structure as laid out above in IMAGINE BEING and you will find yourself gaining confidence, building your unshakable belief system, and taking the actions you need to take to live the life you imagined.

Review Questions for Use Your Personal Power

1. Which of my intentions require my focus?

2. If I do not utilize my power to attain my intentions, what will I get? What will I give up?

3. What questions do I have about the way forward for each of my intentions?

4. Whose help do I need?

CHAPTER 20:

SHARE AND SUSTAIN YOUR ACCOMPLISHMENTS

Those who bring sunshine into the lives of others, cannot keep it from themselves.

—J.M. Barrie

S hare your accomplishment with another person. When you share your journey and its result, you get to focus and pay attention to what actually caused you to be successful (and you may just inspire the other person). It takes a lot to harness your momentum and engage your personal power to accomplish what you want in your life. It takes commitment, dedication, and, at times, perseverance. That's why it is so important to celebrate your accomplishments along the way with the people who have shared the journey with you.

Celebrate the little steps and the giant leaps! Celebrate whether you lose two pounds of your fifty-pound intention, and celebrate again when you lose all fifty pounds. Pop the bubbly when you win the business contract or sell your business. Share the news of your magical date or if you commit to a relationship. Dance when you have cleared one or all of your debts.

Celebrate, celebrate, celebrate! Pay attention to your progress and your successes. Celebration is riddled with energy, creating internal momentum that propels your external actions, and allowing you to spread joy to others. By celebrating, you help yourself as well as encourage and coach others to celebrate their achievements, helping them develop their own energy.

When you coach someone, you get the added benefit of the coaching yourself at the same time—reminding you of your own commitments. You often find that you have had similar experiences to the person you are coaching. Coaching allows you to see your own world and your own point of view in the things going on in your own life. While you are asking questions of the other person, you get to ask yourself the same questions about your own life. This can then give you, as the coach, a new access to an old problem that you have had. As a coach, you are listening to the other person's situation, experiences, and problems, and you are getting to reflect on your own situation, goals, and problems as well.

Have you ever seen someone who has experienced a real personal achievement in some area of his or her life and then go on to become an instructor, teacher, coach, or mentor? A prime example is in one of the hottest shows on TV today: *The Biggest Loser*. Many of the men and women who have participated on that show have gone on to be trainers for their families and communities, sharing what they learned on "the Ranch" with those searching for similar help.

Other examples would be those who gave up unfulfilling jobs as editors and became writers . . . those people who became so proficient at yoga that they became instructors . . . those people who changed their lives to become happy and fulfilled and then later became life coaches . . . those parents who nurtured their children so well and then became great teachers (in schools and communities) . . . or those retired football players who became coaches and managers. These people all got to share their accomplishments continuously by helping others get to where they wanted to be.

The Greatness in You

Too many times we set a goal and can only see the end result. We fail to see that each step along the way is an accomplishment in itself. When you want to lose weight and drop two pounds, it is a big deal! So don't let the ultimate end result rob you of that joy—don't let it creep in and deflate your spirits by telling you that there is still another forty-eight pounds to go. Celebrate what you have just accomplished!

This is, in essence, all about *instant gratification*. While that phrase has garnered a negative reaction in recent years due to the "live for today, pay for it tomorrow" mentality prevalent in today's society, we want you to share the joy of your accomplishments—large and small—and sustain the energy that it can bring to you.

Here's a little secret you might not know: there is greatness in you. If you want to change and be even greater, that is purely up to you and nobody else. So celebrate your greatness. Celebrate who you are—whether you are a mom, dad, brother, sister, aunt, uncle, lover, friend—and what you have accomplished. Put aside the "what is missing" and focus on what you are and what you have done right now.

Share Your Success

When you share with others, not only are you providing some useful experience and information to them, but you are also keeping yourself centered on your commitments and accomplishments. If you share your accomplishment and the process with fifty people, you get to celebrate your accomplishment another fifty times—hooray! It then has you more likely to look at new intentions with more power and energy than you already had.

Now, we talk about all this success and accomplishment, but let's remember that mixed in with the good days are the bad days. On the not-so-good days, you will still be asked to share your experience. It could be you have a committed and scheduled call with someone (a lifeline) and would prefer to do something else or be somewhere else. It's a natural reaction when you are disappointed. But remember that when you share yourself during these times, your whole world is likely to change during your sharing, and, more often than not, you will find yourself in the experience of feeling good again and celebrating your accomplishments once again.

Always remember, sharing:

1. Helps you stay focused on your intentions. If you share your intentions with fifty people, the same people will keep asking you how you are doing with your intention every time they see you.

2. Helps you to sustain momentum. Sharing keeps the review going with yourself on how you are doing with what you set out to accomplish.

3. Helps you get through the not-so-good days. There will be days when you are not feeling focused on your commitments or days when you feel bad about the lack of progress. When you share with others about the not-so-good days, the impact of the disappointment can be taken away by a few friendly smiles, warm hugs, and beneficial advice.

4. Helps you to help others. Sharing your experiences and accomplishments can inspire others into action, even when they have different intentions and goals than yours. The excitement of your accomplishment will give them hope to achieve their goals.

Sustain Your Accomplishments

Once you accomplish some of your intentions, you will notice yourself committing to new ones. The practice here is not just to make new intentions because you have become an intentions junkie. Make sure the new intentions are going to support you and enrich your life. Keeping the energy going when you have accomplished your intentions usually lies in the structure you create.

For instance, when you lose weight, make sure you check in with your nutritionist several times a year to ensure you are still on track, especially if you have struggled with weight issues over the years. When you earn the extra money you had hoped, get some financial advice on how to make the best use of the surplus you have. When you find your life partner, look at the person you need to be to keep the relationship going. When you become fit, keep to the exercise schedule that helps you maintain your fitness.

Accomplishing an intention does not mean that it ends there. Once you do reach a goal, you will be in maintenance mode—you will be looking to make sure you maintain your new life, new you.

Here are some of the ways people keep their structures place:

Diary
Use a diary or calendar to note the milestones. Note the setbacks (to avoid in the future) as well as the accomplishments and times for celebration.

Progress Charts
Use little notebooks or cards to track your progress. Use the ones in the back of this book!

Events
Schedule occasions for the future that keep you focused on your intentions, such as a regular spa day with friends who also want to share their intentions and progress.

Story Boards/Collages
Use pictures, collages, and storyboards that you can look at daily to help you focus and continue your journey with your commitments and intentions. Collect pictures of that new life you want to see— that new home, life partner, career, and so forth. Keep the pictures in a place where you spend at least several minutes each day.

Telephone Calls and Coaching
Use scheduled calls to share your progress with a committed listener. This can be on a weekly or monthly basis (or even daily if that is what it is going to take to get you there).

Committed Listeners

These are people who really are committed to helping you and are willing to give some of their time to talk to you about your commitments and your intentions. You can ask them to do calls with you or you can ask them to meet with you on a regular basis.

Summary

Each day, create the opportunity to celebrate and share your progress. It does not matter if it is a small success or big win. Your achievements matter. You are participating in creating a life you love. It does take effort, and you deserve to be rewarded. To sustain your accomplishment, it will be useful—or may be even necessary—to create structures to maintain your achievement. Have a blast with it!

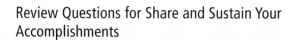

Review Questions for Share and Sustain Your Accomplishments

1. What accomplishment can I celebrate today (small or large) on the road to my imagined life?

2. Who are the two or three people I can share this accomplishment with?

3. How can I keep track of my progress going forward?

PART FIVE:

IMAGINE BEING THE LIGHT

There are two ways of spreading light:
to be the candle or the mirror that reflects it.
Edith Wharton

Thousands of candles can be lit from a single candle,
and the life of the candle will not be shortened.
Buddha

In this section, you will learn to:

- Assess your light
- Spread the light
- Continue the light

CHAPTER 21:

OUR LIGHT

When you possess light within, you see it externally.

—Anaïs Nin

*I*n the first four sections of this book, we asked you to imagine being the cause, the opportunity, the reason, and the energy for a life you love. Mastering those four core concepts will strengthen your inner being and allow you to accomplish anything you want in life.

However, to us, there exists a fifth element that will complete you. It is our contention that being in a life you love means sharing love with those around you. It means being a light to others—your family, your friends, your co-workers, your church, your community, and your world. And what does being the light really mean? Well . . . light is love.

As you imagine being in a life you love and begin living it, you will realize that your light will shine from within. As the true you comes into being, others will notice your "magical presence." Your light will be a reflection of your spirit, your thoughts, your actions, and your beliefs.

Have you ever been in the presence of someone who "feels" serene to you? Who you seem to know even though you've never met? Have you been that person in the room, the one who is at peace and enjoying the moments of the day, whether alone or in the company of others? If you have not previously imagined being a person with a "magical presence," imagine it now. It is possible. You can be that person. Turn your light on, and let it shine.

Kristin's Story

I have been blessed in my life to have had so many people contribute to my growth and well-being. It is a very special experience to have others extend a hand, a word of advice, or simple thoughtfulness. It is because of these many people who have touched me that I wish to give back to others. We do not always see the light in ourselves, and when it is pointed out to us, it beams all around us.

I had a seventh-grade teacher who believed in my writing, and later, my high school grammar teacher called attention to it as well. This helped to develop my belief in myself as it pertained to writing and becoming an author. In college, I had an advisor who suggested I run for president of my sorority while only a sophomore. I had such deep respect for her that I thought if she believed in me, I needed to believe in myself. At the beginning of my business career, I had a managing director invite me to work directly with him, and this instilled in me the courage of my convictions to perform and to grow to levels more quickly than my predecessors in that environment. And my mom is the light in my life. I put her through a lot when I was young, and not once did she waver in her loving support. She is an example of all that is good. Her light is like heaven opening up, and, as a result, she has more love and joy and friendship in her life than a person may be able to imagine!

On a small scale, I have been engaged in helping others realize their vision and expand the scope of their thinking regarding what is possible. I love having this ability and playing this role, and am eager to expand the opportunities for others. I am thrilled when my friends call to ask for advice or even to vent. That they trust me with their personal selves means the world to me. I am eager to help and be needed. Across the miles through phone calls, I support and receive their support. To expand my contribution, I want to participate on a global scale and serve as a conduit and catalyst for achievement and success for individuals, communities, businesses, and, ultimately, nations. I believe that we must own our own lives, yet be responsible citizens. I believe we must continually learn from each other and connect. We need to be skilled in asking for what we need, and in asking ourselves how we can grow. The experiences of my life have prepared me emotionally, socially, and professionally. Am I ready to lead change and lives, and accept that responsibility and accountability? You bet. I have never been more ready.

I want my light to radiate from within, so that others are inspired to shine, too. I love light. I love sunshine. I love mornings. I love the warmth of the rays on my face. I often sit and read or think in the sunlight for hours. It is during this quiet, alone time that I let my mind wander on what I am up to in the world, and whether I am making a contribution. Who am I being for myself and others?

What do I care about every single day? My family and their well-being. I want every joy for each of them, and I want to participate in the creation of it. I care about being self-expressed. As a matter of fact, if I find myself in a situation where I am not self-expressed or my values are compromised, it is not a matter of will I exit, it is a matter of how rapidly. If I am not "on purpose" in my life, I know immediately. Frankly, if I didn't get back on purpose quickly, I fear I'd break my other knee! Not consciously, of course, but the universe has ways of making us pay attention and not all are subtle.

I care deeply about those who do not have the means to care for themselves. I want to shine light on those who need a voice to protect them. I was asked once what would I do if I had $10 million dollars. Among many things, a top priority would be to build an animal care center, so the strays and the abandoned are taken care of. That $10 million would certainly be nice to use for my foundation. What if I did just a little more each day on my plan? Imagine the possibilities.

Something I think about is whether there exists enough time to expand my own rays of sunshine in the lives of others. Will I be remembered? I fondly remember those who have been lights in my life, even if sometimes the light included picking on me. As a child, I was afraid of the dark. I am actually still a little nervous in the dark and with what goes bump in the night. I attribute this to my brother, Kent, who would often sneak into my bedroom and spring up beside my bed with a flashlight under his chin making a big roar. I would be scared and scream, and then just be mad at him for making fun of me. I'd give a million dollars to see his face in the light just one more time.

It is never too soon to be someone's light.

This is a good time to say thank you again to those who serve as my lights. If you don't know who you are, don't worry. Part of spreading light is acknowledging when it is received and paying it forward. I will be in touch to spread the light you've shared with me. You are part of who I am and imagine being.

Jaqui's Story

There are many people who have been the light for me to become who I am today. I have gratefully received mentoring, coaching, and advice from a number of generous people.

I was born into a working-class family who were very generous with their love and guidance. I had some very good schoolteachers who pushed me to pay attention and learn. I worked hard in my first job after graduation, and I disciplined myself to learn as much as I could. At work, I asked lots of questions and requested help. People would shine their light on me and help me. It was magnificent. Throughout my career, I stepped out of my comfort zone to get what I needed to move on powerfully with my life. In doing so, I reciprocated the help given to me by being available and being the light for others. When people have asked for my help, I have generally given it. I am aware that I cannot be all things to all people and that I cannot help everyone. However, where I can be, I enjoy being the light for others and them being the light for me. I am eternally grateful for that.

I once met a person begging for money in the train station. He asked me for money. I asked him how much he had himself. He took from his pocket a handful of silver coins. I think there was about £2.50 in his hand in total. I took it from him to see what he would do, and then I said "thank you." He just looked at me, astonished. I waited a minute or two to see what he would do, how he would react. He just stood there looking confused. I put his £2.50 in my purse. He then started smiling. Eventually I gave him a £5 note. Why did I do this? I wanted to see how he would treat me if I took his money—since he wanted mine. He was okay with me, although he was puzzled at first. At the time, it felt like he was willing to give me what he had, that he was saying "Okay, if your need is greater than mine, then fair enough." It was rather a weird experiment, and I don't know why I did it other than to see how he would react. However, before the interaction with him I had noticed him walk up to a very tall gentleman who was wearing a long colourful scarf. This man seemed preoccupied and didn't interact with the guy who was begging. I guess I was observing how I, too, ignore people who are begging, and also recognized my own fear around such people.

After my interaction, the tall guy made an effort to approach me and ask me who I was. It was all very strange. I just replied that I was no one in particular, just someone waiting for a train to take her home. He asked me to look after his bags while he made a call (a very stupid thing to do I know, but I did it.) When he returned, he proceeded to give me his name and address. It turned out that he was one of the vets at Newmarket (a famous UK horse-racing venue). He told me that he had a ranch in Bermuda, and if ever I wanted to have a vacation there to just give him a call. How amazing was that! The whole experience was as if something magical had happened. Something that was out of the ordinary. I had chosen to connect with strangers and I had an amazing experience. Here I was having interrupted the expected pattern with a beggar, and having a stranger walking over to me and contributing something to me. How incredible! I have had many experiences like this one in my life, and I call them "my experiments." I thoroughly enjoy reaching out to people and seeing how others reach out back.

I remember my friend Barbro, a fiercely independent woman from Sweden, telling me how difficult she found being open to others contributing to her life. Barbro said that she agreed to do an experiment on herself on a journey from San Diego to London. She had some very heavy luggage and found it hard to lift it all, although she normally would have managed it. However, on this occasion, she made a pledge with herself not to lift the cases from the time she left her home in San Diego until her arrival in London. Barbro was amazed by how many people offered to help her lift and move her luggage along her journey, often without her having to ask. They just came up to her and asked if they could help her.(Of course, she had sent out smiles and looked helplessly at her luggage.) Barbro then realized something: In the past, there had been many occasions where people had offered to help her and she had responded quite quickly, "No thanks, I can manage." What was that all about? *I can manage.* Of course we can manage, but isn't it nice when someone offers to help us, too—when we allow them to contribute to us!

We are all so appreciative when someone reaches out to us to guide us on our way. There are people who step in just when we need them— when we are about to make a mistake, take a wrong turn, or engage in inappropriate actions. There are people who give up their time, their energy, or their resources to provide a helping hand. We are sometimes privileged, even overwhelmed, by their kindness.

If you have never had this experience yourself, then it is time to allow people to be this kind of contribution to you. Accept the help of others when it is offered and ask for it when it is not. We, in turn, can be that for those we want to contribute to. Often it is a matter of creating occasions and opportunities to provide help. Day to day and moment to moment, we can look for those opportunities for us to be the light for one another.

Summary

We believe that to be complete—to be all that we can imagine being—includes being a light to others. We are all gifted with the ability to make a difference in the world by our words and actions. Sometimes, it is a matter of just reaching out.

Remember, too, that as you stretch your hand to others, be sure to grasp those that are extended to you. We sometimes fail to accept contributions from those who want to help us, those family members, friends, and associates who see a need in us and want to be there to help us along in our journey. Accept their light as you would hope others would accept yours.

CHAPTER 22:

YOUR LIGHT

We cannot hold a torch to light another's path without brightening our own.

—Ben Sweetland

We are in glorious wonderment when we look at all the people we know who have been the light for us. The same people who are being useful to us are also contributing to others, too. There is a spirit of reciprocation going on with our neighbors, friends, colleagues, families, and communities, all working together every day.

We may not know who is providing what help outside of our own networks, but this we do know: so many lives are being touched by this spirit of generosity. We are in wonderment when we realize the contributions being made. We believe that if we did a global audit of how many people are assisting others, the numbers would astound us.

While we do not hear about all the efforts going on everywhere—usually only those that seem out of the ordinary get the attention—we understand that even the small offerings of help ultimately make a huge difference in the world at large.

Think of those who have great meaning in your life. What did they do to earn that place in your heart? Can you imagine how you would feel if someone acknowledged you as the person who has played a role in being a light in his or her life?

There are many possibilities, great and small, to touch others. Think of the stories of the anonymous Santa Claus who donates to an orphanage each year, or the granddaughter who reads to the elderly at the nursing home on Sundays. Think of those whose phone call or card arrived to you just in the nick of time, letting you know you were being thought of—that someone cared. Think of those who you immediately reach out to call when you have joy or pain. How wonderful and simple and free it is to be there for another person.

Kathleen's Story

Consider the story of Kathleen.

I was born in Coffeyville, Kansas. I loved growing up on a farm with a big family—nine children, although one passed away in infancy. We did not have much financially, but none of us children knew that at the time. We did have boundless love and support.

Education was especially important in my family. My father had dropped out of high school when influenza was sweeping across the country, taking thousands of lives. He read all he could, and he wanted his children to learn. So each of us kids went to college, except for one who was successful in the Army and worked for an airline afterward.

I always wanted to be a teacher. I guess that's why I liked to play school. My mother had been a teacher before she married, but like many women in that time, once she married she no longer worked. She took care of the home and the children. She and my father dated a long time before they married because they knew her job would end when they did.

I had many happy experiences with my mother, writing papers while she made hot chocolate and helped me with my spelling. I loved to learn (and still do). That's what led me to teaching. I taught in one high school for twenty-six years, and two additional years in another town. If I had to guess, I would say that I taught approximately 4,000 students.

Among other classes, I taught college preparatory classes. I wanted to ensure that my students were ready for the next stage, that they could compete at a high level. I wanted them to be well-spoken and confident, and I hope that I was a good teacher to them as I worked very hard at my craft. I always tried to be well-prepared, organized, and on time as I wanted those young people to emulate what they saw.

I loved my students, the teaching staff, and the administration. I loved my career. Education makes you more interested—and interesting—and broadens so many horizons. It makes you a student of the world. I've been fortunate to have traveled to twenty-nine countries. During my travels, I developed an appreciation for art, and was excited to see many famous museums throughout Europe. I loved traveling, and I appreciated everything I got to do.

I am also appreciative that my husband, Bob, loved what he did, too, which was in conservation. Bob and I had attended the same high school, but we did not actually start dating until two years after graduation. We have been married since 1964, and he is still my sweetheart.

While I have been fortunate, I have also had my share of life's setbacks. I am a survivor of breast cancer, and my husband is a survivor of kidney cancer. The worst part of going through the cancer was the unknown, mainly for my daughters and other family members, who were frequently at my side during my recovery, reading to me, or placing a blanket over me, or questioning the doctors—basically just loving me. As I regained my health, I came to truly better appreciate my doctors, my family, my books, and my life. I also appreciated my girlfriends, who saw me through the bouts of chemo and did not let my sense of wit and humor fade despite the circumstances.

The cancer was an interruption, but nothing has gotten in the way of my dreams. I can honestly say that no dreams were ever put on hold. The cancer treatment might have kept me from going to the theater, one of my favorite things, but that was a temporary thing. Now, as we experience more illness in the family—my brother-in-law—we are sad and feeling vulnerable, but we accept what we are facing as we have great faith and children to help. That's what families do.

I have excellent role models in my life, including my parents, who were tremendous people. They have always been the lights in my life. My mother died just short of age 100, not many years ago. I would help with her care-giving—again, this is what families do. My father was a kind and giving man. When a farmer he knew was killed in an accident, my dad used his combine to help bring in that farmer's crops before he did his own. That's what we saw growing up. You helped everybody. You didn't get paid for it. It's what you did. We grew up seeing this, and that's what the value was. It is what we were taught. I'll never inherit much money, but I have a tremendous inheritance from my parents. My brothers and sisters and I were blessed to grow up as we did.

My immediate family has more than 100 members, and the reunions are large! I once baked 600 cookies for one! My nephew and his family hosted a weekend family gathering they called Pumpkin Creek Days, and some people were surprised that so many people could get along without drinking. My family has a great sense of humor, and they are the epitome of community.

That sense of giving back to others has remained with me and my family all our lives. Today, Bob and I are American Cancer Society drivers who take patients to treatments in nearby towns. On those drives, we listen . . . and listen. We take patients wherever they need to go. We also visit people in nursing homes and volunteer at the hospital and church. I am also a member of Pink Ribbon Pals, a breast cancer survivor group.

I "pray like the Dickens" and keep three lists to direct prayers. I also keep
busy in an investment club, two bridge clubs and a book club. I do yoga;
I know that the most stressful times—when you do not feel like breathing,
stretching, or exercising—is exactly when you need it most.

Is my life as I imagined it would be? I didn't plan my life out and outline
my life. It just fell into place. Is that weird? I don't think I really planned
what I wanted, but I have been very blessed with wonderful kids, great
sons-in-law, and a loving husband. What more would you want? Our faith is
a given, but family and friends are what you have in your life.

As for what's next, I am just going to keep on doing what I'm doing. We
are happy, and we are grateful for what we have.

Be the Light

As a teacher, Kathleen shared her light with thousands of students,
ensuring that they received the best education available in order to
step out confidently into the world. And that spirit of giving has always
extended to other areas of her life as well, a lasting tribute to values
instilled in her by her parents.

One of the best methods of feeling better about where and who
we are is to give of our voice, our time, or our thoughts. You have the
opportunity every day to touch some else's heart . . . to be a light.

Just as you actively cause change in your life, you can do so for others.
Speak up when you see a wrong, and help to make it right. We have
come to a point in time when we turn the other cheek when we should
be looking headlong into the realities. When a child or animal is hurt,
take a stand. When you have a resource to share—words of wisdom and
encouragement, a book, a class, a donation—do it *if it feels right to you*.
Being the light should not feel like an obligation, and you shouldn't
participate just to please others. Being the light must come from a place
of authenticity. You need to want to do what you will choose to do.

Do you have people in your life who would add you to their lifeline
list of or identify you as a Super Champion for one of their intentions?
Are you choosing to play that role for anyone? There is no need to wait
to be asked. Just decide the light you wish to be. If you are currently a
light to someone but want to do more, just get started.

How can you be a light to someone else? There are so many ways:

> A smile
> A please or thank you
> A helping hand
> A rose from your garden
> A letter of thanks and gratitude
> A piece of useful information

A connection
A direction
A road map
A cup of tea
A penny or a pound
A chunk of your time
A share of your life
A drive to the beach, zoo, or park
A story or a poem
A joke
A lesson
A piece of advice or some coaching

You have opportunities every day to spread your light from wherever you are. Your moments of light can happen:

At social networking sites
At community or family gatherings
At associations, charities, or church
At school, university, or college
At playgroups, moms and tots, day-care
At clubs (sports, health, leisure)
At parties and celebrations
At social events
At business events and conferences
At the airport and on the aircraft
On the bus or train
At the queue (in line)
At the park, shops, or supermarket
At the doctor's office, dentist's office, or health center

It is often said that it can take one of life's critical events to wake us up to what is important. We need not wait for big events or experiences before we take action to improve our own life and the lives of others. The kind of contribution that we truly want to make someday, one day, is the kind of contribution we can make *today*. Small steps can cover a lot of ground.

You should note, too, that you cannot be all things to all people. You will get to please some and not others. You may find that the exact way someone wanted to be contributed to is not how you are prepared to contribute, and it will be another setback for you to get through. It's the nature of life. It's the ebb and the flow. Your contribution will be accepted by some and not by others. It is your choice and also their choice. Don't let it stop you from being the contribution to those who are only too pleased to receive it! There is no point in wasting energy where it isn't wanted or accepted. Move on and leave the experience behind—with them, not with you. Learn to forgive and forget, keep learning, and keep practicing. It takes some skill in letting go of some of the experiences you have in assisting others—who responds well, not so well, or even indifferently. No matter how far you have come on your journey, you'll have bright and not-so-bright days. As you manage the setbacks that will ping you, focus on the light . . . your light.

More often than not, people will welcome you and what you are offering. We do need each other. Let's just join hands . . . and let our light shine.

Will you imagine being the light? It is your life. Your story.

Summary

Being a light to someone else does not need to come in the form of a grand gesture. It's the little things that can add up to the most joy in the life of another. Think of the everyday things you can do to bring some light into the life of someone who needs it. Think of the places where you believe there are people in need, and dedicate yourself to spending time there. As others have been a light to you, be a light unto others.

Review Questions for Your Light

1. What and who do you care about?

2. What and who can you affect today? What do you choose to be or do?

3. Who can you love?

4. What have you to offer and what are you prepared to give that could be of use to someone else?

CHAPTER 23:

SPREAD THE LIGHT

Do all the good you can, and make as little fuss about it as possible.

—Charles Dickens

*I*magine . . . you are a young child, with little shelter to keep you warm from the cold and a constant ache in your stomach from hunger. The surroundings hills separate you from warring nations, you walk amid thousands just like you, and your parents died of AIDS before reaching age thirty. Your goal, each and every day of your life, is to find nourishment— one meal that will sustain you to face the next uncertain day.

Imagine . . . a stranger makes a donation from his computer in Iowa. Grain is harvested in a field manned by volunteers, brave truck drivers traverse the terrain to reach the camp, and your hands deliver that meal. Imagine that child sharing it with his sister.

Now imagine this.

You are frightened, cowering in a corner of your house as a voice rages out of control. Your body is battered and bruised; your spirit is broken. You hide in silence, not able to tell your friends, your family, or your co-workers what awaits you each day you step through the door to your own home.

Imagine . . . your friend finally "sees" you and gives you no choice in intervention. She takes over. She leads you to safety. She was never asked. You heal and use your voice to speak out and save another life.

Now imagine this.

You have been told that the lack of energy you have been feeling is due to a cancer that is coursing through your body. You have only months to live, hours quickly ticking by in which you must figure out how your young children will be cared for, how your husband will manage without you, and how you will cope with your own mortality.

Imagine . . . your pastor reaches out to his congregation. A retired, widowed hospice worker steps forward to re-apply her skills. She knows loss and steps in to talk with you, to reassure you, to adopt your family, and to help with the transition. She becomes an extension of you. You are peaceful.

Being the light is not only about the large-scale issues of the world. It is also about your neighbor, your neighborhood, your community, and your brothers and sisters. The measure of a life is not based on what items you amass in the world, but on the individuals you touch. There are grand gestures, and the opportunity to serve someone's daily needs. You can build schools in South Africa or smile at a person in the street. You can pay for a college education or you can pick up the phone to check on a friend with the flu. You can adopt a child or volunteer at the community center. You can donate a million dollars or host a "Single Shower" for your unmarried friend. You can recognize when someone is in need . . . and help.

There is a saying that there are two ways of spreading light in the world: to be the candle or the mirror that reflects it. Today, throughout the world, millions of people are looking for those lights to help them through darkness. Their darkness can be extreme, or it can simply be the help they need to deal with the anxiety of just being in the world. As you imagine being the light, consciously consider who may need your light. Was there a time when you received a phone call out of the blue, from someone who was just thinking about you? That felt good, right? Imagine that. Become *present* to how simple it can be to impact a person's life, to create meaningful memories, and to connect with one another.

We believe that, as beings in this world, we are all connected and we are all designed to reach out to others. Sometimes these people will be less fortunate than we are. Sometimes they will be just like us. Sometimes they will be people we perceive to be better or more advanced or more affluent. No one is exempt from the stuff of life, and no one needs to take on darkness alone.

Make a Connection

Earlier in the book, we shared the concept, "If we are not in the presence of life, we are not present to it." Meaning, if we are not experiencing something firsthand, we are not considering that other people may be, and as a result, may be in need.

And today there is so much need. So many of us are trying to feel our significance in a world of significant happenings—families being separated due to soldiers going to war, the economy rattling our security, and the strife and struggle that comes with trying to keep our homes, our jobs, and our lives together.

What we are searching for—and even hunting for—is connection. In the movie *Crash*, Don Cheadle's character says, "I think we miss that touch so much, that we *crash* into each other, just so we can feel something."

The significance of connecting with others lies in the understanding that we are not alone in the world. We may live independent lives from one another, but there are experiences, situations, and beliefs that help us understand each other and be understood. We need each other and we need to recognize that there are so many opportunities to connect to others, some as effortless as smiling or opening a door.

And by "connect," we mean spirit to spirit. Connection can happen instantly, in person or even by phone or e-mail. These are the times when we feel safe to share the essence of ourselves—our values and beliefs, our concerns and our fears—in a very short window of time. Some people call these experiences "soul" experiences. These are the connections that happen at the core.

Let's share those stories. We can change the state of our lives by changing what we place our attention on. As we give of ourselves and step up to better our lives and the lives of others, there is a ripple effect. It is passed on, often in ways we are not even aware of. It is light.

Let's eliminate the "not mine" syndrome and create the "What if?" mentality as individuals and communities of people. We have the potential to create a groundswell, a surge of ownership for being the light for ourselves and others.

Make a Difference

We truly believe that all of us, in some way, want to make a contribution to the world. It may be in the words we write, the music we compose, the people we teach, the bodies we heal, the homes we build, or the hearts we touch. Sometimes, we just don't know how we can reach out to others.

One of our goals is to unite those of you who want to make a difference in the lives of others through our *Imagine Being* Community. We want to bring together individuals from around the world to share their ideas, passions, and resources in one online community that is devoted to reaching out to those in need. We want to share the stories of those who imagine a better life and world . . . those who are willing to help them realize those dreams . . . and those who have the knowledge to connect all of us.

If you would like to join us as a member in the *Imagine Being* Community, visit www.ImagineBeing.com for information. Together, we can make a difference. We can shift our collective consciousness to the positive energy resulting from these connections.

Your light. Their light. Our light. Imagine being.

Summary

We believe that a complete being is one who shines a light in someone else's life. There are millions of people out there who need help, who are waiting for someone to lend a hand, offer a shoulder, or provide physical and emotional nourishment. Be the light.

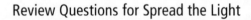

Review Questions for Spread the Light

1. Who are lights in your life and what role has each played?

2. What is the value of connecting?

3. What light have you received today? What light have you given?

4. Who will you connect with today?

CHAPTER 24:

CONTINUE THE LIGHT

If you wish to experience peace, provide peace for one another.
—Tenzin Gyatso, the 14th Dalai Lama

There are many stories to share about who have been lights for you and the ways you have shined your light. Tell those stories! You are not bragging when you let someone know you served dinner at church or fed a stray cat or babysat for a single mom. You are letting others know that they can step up, too. In sharing these stories, you give to others ideas of what they can be or do. We so often want to extend a hand, but are not sure as to how to go about doing it.

On the *Imagine Being* web site, we will share stories of people who have been the light to others. Their stories—the grand gestures and simple kindnesses—will show the role we play in the lives of others.

Imagine the extent to which we can participate in helping each other and, in doing so, help ourselves. Much of what we read and hear about today concerns the mistakes we make as human beings. Yet we have the opportunity to share the good stories of how we connect with each other. We can do—and be—good.

There is an opportunity to read and learn about the intentions of others in being a light to others.

Kristin's Intentions

I have given a lot of thought to how I might go about declaring my intentions around being the light. It occurs to me that being the light for others is very congruent with my life purposes. My purpose in this life is threefold: 1) to consciously connect people through the process of giving and receiving; 2) to lead nations and people to peace through my pen and my voice; and 3) to liberate the power of women—beginning in the heart and home—to live *on purpose* through clarity of intention and by leveraging the opportunities available to them.

My intentions regarding being the light include being a better listener, and utilizing what I learn about the stories of others to help people realize that we are never alone and what we struggle with is not unique to us. We're in this life together. I will also share the stories of the simple tokens and the miraculous. I will keep writing, and I will use my voice to speak and teach.

Within the next seven years of my life, I will create a non-profit foundation with the goal of consciously connecting people through the process of giving and receiving. Within this context, I will provide an opportunity for women to live their lives on purpose through creating and leading business or social projects that resolve local or global issues, instigate change and conversation, engage communities of action, generate revenue streams for targeted causes, leverage power at a grassroots level while attracting the attention of corporations and governments as appropriate, and create and provide a platform from which to share these efforts for use by other women. This foundation will generate a ripple effect of leadership, ownership, participation, and caring for country and community.

It is about time I stepped up and practiced what I preach about LIP service—Living in Possibility. Boy, talk about boxing myself in . . . I've just declared this intention to you as reader. Now to follow through.

Jaqui's Intentions

Being the light for me is about providing others with a way of moving forward in their lives. If they find themselves in a rut, then I look at how I can help them see through where they are stuck and where I can I assist them in working their way out of their rut. I like to be the light for people who are seeing their world through the "glass half empty" mentality; I want to shine the light on them so they can see their life through the "glass half full." I expect that I will assist at least as many people in the next few decades as I have helped in the past two, helping them find and realize their possibilities for what they imagine that being for them.

When I think back to that time when I was ill, I truly believe that experience helped me to see how it is, or how it can be, for people who feel so desperate. Everyone, including me, needs to be "the light." We have much to give to one another without giving away too much of what we need for ourselves. There are so many ways we can help one another, and yet it is often hard to contribute to someone or be contributed to by others. Why?

Maybe we have learned to be too independent, too self-directed, too self-reliant? Jolly good show! Awesome! No need to worry about him or her; they can handle everything, they never ask for anything, they never need a hand. Bah, humbug! We all need a hand! All of us! No exceptions. There is a myth of being self-reliant and independent. Sure, be this when you need to be, and then when you need a helping hand, reach out! There is always someone there. Really, there is.

The thought of not needing a hand or asking for it might come from the thought that if I don't ask them, then they won't ask me. Or maybe it's because there are so many problems in the world like hunger, cancer, poverty, war, and disease that we cannot cope with the magnitude of it all. Good reason, good enough explanation, good excuse. There, it's all too big for me to handle, so someone else bigger than me (the political leaders, the government, community leaders, business leaders) will need to sort it all out. Of course, they all do have a part to play, and so do we, as citizens of the world. We can be the light for others in many different ways. Even a smile at a complete stranger on the train or the bus goes a long way. I once walked along Oxford Street, one of the busiest streets in London, and I did a little experiment. I said to my friend, "Let's walk down the street and look at everyone we pass by and smile and see how many smiles we get back." We were astonished. Nearly every person smiled back. It was truly amazing. There were hundreds of people all smiling back. Fantastic!

To be the light for others you need to really *want* to be the light—there is no *should* involved. There is no need to do anything you don't want to do. However, most people care enough about something to want to be the light for it. People care about kids, about education, about the elderly, about animals, about sports, about other concerns such as hunger, poverty, and disease. Find out what you care about most. What links you to your values the most? Once you discover what it is, it is relatively easy to be the light for others.

I care about people finding ways of getting out of the ruts they are in to empower themselves. For me, this can be people in my hometown or overseas in South Africa (where I have done volunteer work). It doesn't matter to me where the people live; the same help is offered, over here or over there, for people to see how they can create more of what they need for themselves.

As I get older, I care more about people facing cancer and old age. This, in part, is due to my mum suffering from cancer—seeing what I saw and feeling how I felt. Seeing how incredible she was at handling the disease, and her own mortality, makes me want to help others facing the same challenges. I also want to help family members who are getting older and coping with the various setbacks that come with the aging process.

I care about the different ways in which I can make a difference to a variety of people who come into my life. I like the term *make yourself useful* and the idea that if all of us thought this way, then the people of the world would have a better chance of causing a real change on a global level. People do want to help other people. It's just that not all people want to help all the time.

I make it my choice to offer myself on a voluntary basis as a coach for several people each year. I do this because I want to, and I do it with people who I believe will pass on the contribution to others, people I believe want to be useful to others and give others a helping hand along the way. I do not expect others who coach to do this, although I know of many who do. It isn't a hardship for me because I love coaching. It is the time commitment that is the hardest thing about it as I give the voluntary coaching as much attention as I would a client. I expect when I stop coaching for a living, I will still live to coach. I expect I might work with teenagers on a voluntary basis or I may work with the elderly. I expect to keep contributing and make myself useful, being a light for others wherever I can in whatever small way.

Summary

There are opportunities waiting for you to continue to spread the light. If you feel inclined to share your intentions of the contributions you wish to bring to others, join the *Imagine Being* Community. The more we bring light into the lives of others, the more we all benefit.

✦ IMAGINE BEING

We titled this book *Imagine Being* for a reason: to let you know that you have the right to **imagine** a life different from what you are now living—that imagination is the most powerful tool you have for living a life *with* purpose and *on* purpose; and to show you that **being** that person you have always dreamed of is within reach—that creating the real you, the one you have always wanted to be, is attainable through the principles included in this book.

We know that because we have lived it. The personal stories we have shared are proof that we have stumbled, we have fallen, we have made mistakes, but we have also persevered and succeeded in turning our lives around. We are now living lives we love by employing the same principles we have shared with you.

Imagine Being is, above all, about putting your dreams into action, making the impossible possible and the unreal real. You have the power within you to create the life you imagine for yourself. It starts with giving thought to what you believe will make you happier. You have the capacity to design a future for yourself—one that ignites the passion within you and excites you (and those around you). When you adhere to the thoughts and follow the steps outlined in this book, we believe you will be closer to realizing your future by design, rather than leading a life left to chance.

Opportunities for living the lives we truly love are available to all of us. All we need to do is wake up to what is within our reach. Even when we find it hard to believe, we sometimes need to take a leap of faith that the opportunities will show up. When we set about creating something new, we may have to learn different ways of doing things. We may need to summon up the courage to face the setbacks in our way and be resilient in turning them aside. Then again, we may be surprised at how easy it is to achieve the intentions we've declared for ourselves.

In writing this book, we, the authors, have had to learn new things and overcome a number of difficulties and setbacks. We learned to keep going even when we had our reasons, explanations, and excuses for stopping from time to time. We came to understand in this process that intentions require focus and attention. Without these, our intentions are merely daydreams and fantasies.

Focus and attention require constant actions, constant momentum. Without actions, there are no results. Our lives are carved out by the actions we take or do not take. Our actions are created from our thoughts about the life that we imagine for ourselves. It begins with imagination . . . that turns into possibilities . . . that turns into opportunities . . . that turns into actions . . . that ends in desired results.

New Year's Eve

It is New Year's Eve as we write these closing thoughts. It is both an ending and a beginning. Another year has passed, one that, for us, has ended with the realization of a dream—to pass on our insights and experiences for finding a life you love. In the coming year, we hope to hear of your stories—how the principles we have shared here have changed your lives for the better.

No matter what time of year you pick up this book, we wish you the following as you begin your journey to imagining a life you love:

- ◆ May you claim ownership of your life.
- ◆ May you know that you are never alone.
- ◆ May you grab the opportunities that arise.
- ◆ May you realize that the setbacks are temporary.
- ◆ May you stand tall in your beliefs.
- ◆ May you keep moving forward.
- ◆ May you love and laugh and share your light.

May you say to yourself, "Today is my day, as is every day from here forward. Each is mine to create, each is mine to cause. No matter what the winds of change bring, I have within me all that is necessary to imagine being in a life I love. This is my story, my moment, my life. I am the reason and the energy behind my progress and my contribution. I have a light within that is splendid and will be shared. This is the beginning of my purpose in being all that I am."

Our hope for you is that you take our challenge to be the author of your own life and be responsible for creating the life that you imagine for yourself.

We wish you happiness and fulfillment in all that you imagine being.

And we hope that someday soon, you will *be in a life you love*.

APPENDIX: WORKBOOK

WELCOME!

Welcome to the companion workbook for *Imagine Being in a Life You Love*!

We are glad that you have decided to take responsibility for creating the life you truly desire. As you progress through the exercises in this workbook, you will strengthen the core of your being by identifying those areas within you that give you the power to realize your dreams.

- You, being the *cause* of designing your life

- You, being the *opportunity* maker in your life

- You, being the *reason* for momentum in your life

- You, being the *energy* responsible for your life

- You, being the *light* that guides the way for others

To reconfirm your commitment to creating that life, please declare your intention:

I will participate in my own life.

_____

(Sign here)

_____

(Date)

So, if you are ready to begin, let's get started!

✦ INTRODUCTION

This is what we know about what happens in the process of living: When we are not in the presence of it, we are not present to it. As humans, we often put off designing the lives we love until it is too late. We tend to believe that we have all the time in the world—although our time here is finite. The time to begin authoring the design of your life is now. Don't put off to tomorrow what you must be considering today, whether it is attention to your children, health, marriage, finances, spirituality, or other need. Your time has come to actively participate in your own life.

THE PAST

What did I imagine for myself as a child?

_____

_____

_____

_____

_____

_____

What did I imagine for myself as a teen?

_____

_____

_____

_____

_____

What actions did I take to create the life I wanted?

_____

_____

_____

_____

_____

_____

What was the result of my actions? Did I follow through on them? Did I stop? Why?

_____

_____

_____

_____

THE PRESENT

On a scale of 1 to 5 (with 5 being the best), how do I rate my life today? Why?

_____

_____

_____

_____

Who am I today?

_____

_____

_____

Where am I today?

_____

_____

_____

Is my life what I imagined it would be? If not, why?

_____

_____

_____

_____

_____

What is working in my life?

_____

_____

_____

_____

What is not working in my life?

_____

_____

_____

What is missing in my life?

_____

_____

_____

Is there something I specifically imagine for myself at this stage of my life?

_____

_____

_____

_____

THE FUTURE

What do I imagine for myself in the future?

_____

_____

_____

_____

What would make me happier?

_____

_____

_____

_____

_____

Do I see what I imagine for myself as possible or a pipedream? (Be as clear as possible about each of the following areas.)

Family:_____

_____

Career:_____

_____

Faith: _____

_____

Health: _____

_____

Other: _____

_____

What would it take to make these things happen?

_____

_____

_____

_____

_____

What immediate actions can I take?

_____

_____

_____

_____

✦ PART ONE: IMAGINE BEING THE CAUSE

Many people feel that life just happens to them, and it will, unless you cause the events, the situations, the opportunities, and the miracles you wish to manifest in your life. You have to remember that you do cause the not-so-great stuff, too. Your choices impact the direction of your life. That's why it is critical that you take responsibility for your choices. Even in the worst of times, when you want to blame others, you must acknowledge that you played a role in it, large or small. Owning your responsibility for who you are and how you turn up in the world is a giant leap toward realizing that you are the cause of being where and what you are.

What am I willing to cause or create in my own life?

_____

_____

_____

_____

What am I taking responsibility for in my life?

_____

_____

_____

_____

Where am I assigning responsibility to someone or something else for things in my life?

_____

_____

_____

_____

Assessing Your Life

If I were free to choose and knew that I could not fail, what would I choose for myself?

_____

_____

_____

What is really stopping me from making these choices? Is it that I am fearful to make them? Is it that I don't know how to go about making them happen? How can I progress with what I would really choose?

_____

_____

_____

On a scale of 1 to 5 (with 5 being the best), how do I rate my happiness in the following areas?

1. Health _____   5. Job _____

2. Fitness _____   6. Family _____

3. Love _____   7. Relaxation _____

4. Relationships _____

Where do I need to focus attention?

Health _____

Fitness _____

Love _____

Relationships _____

Job _____

Family _____

Relaxation _____

Is there anyone I need to talk to about the changes I see for myself in the areas I have identified?

Health _____

Fitness _____

Love _____

Relationships _____

Job _____

Family _____

Relaxation _____

What (if anything) do I need to forgive myself for with what I have done/not done in the past?

_____

_____

_____

_____

What (if anything) do I need to forgive others for with what they have done/not done in the past?

_____

_____

_____

_____

What mistakes have I made that I am now willing to accept and learn from?

_____

_____

_____

_____

Am I using TEMP excuses to keep me from doing what I truly desire? If so, how?

Time _____

Energy _____

Money _____

People _____

Define Who and Where You Want to Be

How would I define happiness if I were talking to a friend?

_____

_____

_____

_____

How will I take responsibility for my own happiness from this day forward?

_____

_____

_____

_____

How do I spend most of my time, energy, and money? With whom do I spend most of my time?

Time

_____

_____

_____

Energy

_____

_____

_____

Money

_____

_____

_____

People

_____

_____

_____

From what I listed above, what is revealed about where I seem to be placing my commitments? Are these commitments conscious commitments, habits, or duties and obligations?

_____

_____

_____

What do I need to stop doing?

_____

_____

_____

_____

What am I dissatisfied with most in my life?

_____

_____

_____

_____

_____

Use the Change Equation—$D > (V + K + C)$—to evaluate your resistance to this change.

My dissatisfaction:

_____

_____

_____

My vision for what I want in life:

_____

_____

_____

My steps for attaining that vision:

_____

_____

_____

The costs or consequences of my change:

_____

_____

_____

Create a Lifeline

Who are the five people I can ask to be my lifelines?

1. _____
2. _____
3. _____
4. _____
5. _____

What do I want my lifelines to help me focus on?

Family:_____

Career:_____

Faith: _____

Health: _____

Other: _____

_____

List why these areas are important to you.

Family:_____

Career:_____

Faith: _____

Health: _____

Other: _____

_____

What can my lifelines personally do to help me in these areas?

Family:_____

Career:_____

Faith: _____

Health: _____

Other: _____

_____

PART TWO: IMAGINE BEING THE OPPORTUNITY

You will begin to realize that the possibilities for your life and your contributions in the world are whatever you choose to create. Then once you begin to "dream," you must attain focus. Letting your imagination run wild is exactly what you should do. Once it has galloped through sea, desert, and land, rein it in and really focus on what you imagined, and then how you will make it possible. Creating opportunities is not a difficult task. You must be willing to put yourself out there. What feels like a risk is likely not that much of a risk at all. Better to have tried and been turned down than to not have tried.

Take Advantage of the Big O

What possibilities do I see for myself?

Family:_____

Career:_____

Faith: _____

Health: _____

Other: _____

If there were no limitations, what opportunities would I seek for myself?

_____

_____

_____

_____

_____

_____

Where might I look for new opportunities?

_____

_____

_____

_____

_____

_____

Are there any reasons, excuses, or explanations that I have that are getting in the way of my possibilities?

_____

_____

_____

_____

Who can I talk to about the opportunities that might be available to me?

_____

_____

_____

_____

Where can I go to do research for my possibilities (library, Internet, networks, and associations)?

_____

_____

_____

_____

When I look at the opportunities, what problems do I see in creating them?

_____

_____

_____

_____

_____

Am I willing to confront the problems? If not, why?

_____

_____

_____

_____

_____

If not, am I willing to seek help?

_____

_____

_____

_____

What boundaries have I put in place that will not allow me to have the life I love?

_____

_____

_____

_____

What am I saying to others and myself about the circumstances I find myself in today?

_____

_____

_____

_____

If I am I willing to create the opportunities despite my circumstances, how will I go about it?

_____

_____

_____

_____

What obstacles do I see when I look at creating opportunities in my life? What opportunities have I imagined that I have not taken because of the fear or concern for the risk that they bring?

_____

_____

_____

_____

What courageous actions do I need to take now?

_____

_____

_____

_____

As of one year from today, what do I want my life to look like?

_____

_____

_____

_____

_____

_____

_____

_____

_____

_____

_____

Be the Author of Your Possibilities

What do I believe is possible?

_____

_____

_____

How do I want to invest my time?

_____

_____

_____

_____

What skills and talents do I have?

_____

_____

_____

_____

_____

If I could transform myself and my life, how would I feel each day?

_____

_____

_____

_____

How will I go about creating my possibility?

_____

_____

_____

_____

What do I already have that helps me create my possibilities?

_____

_____

_____

_____

What else might I need?

_____

_____

_____

_____

How can I alter my behavior, thoughts, and actions to achieve what I want?

_____

_____

_____

_____

_____

What can I read and who can I talk to keep me focused on my possibilities?

_____

_____

_____

_____

_____

Who inspires me in the way they create their own possibilities? Can I talk to these people or read about them?

_____

_____

_____

_____

_____

Declare Your Intentions

On a scale of 1 to 5 (with five being the highest), how committed am I to my intentions? If less than 5, why?

_____

_____

_____

_____

_____

_____

What are my Top 5 intentions for the coming year? (I need to write out in a specific way what I want to create for myself, how I will make it happen, the intended result, and the time frame for it.)

1. _____

_____

2. _____

_____

3. _____

_____

4. _____

_____

5. _____

_____

How will I be flexible, adaptable, and maybe even courageous in making these five things happen for myself?

_____

_____

_____

_____

_____

_____

What Super Champions do I want sitting at my roundtable?

_____

_____

_____

_____

_____

_____

Here is my round table. (Draw it here.):

What questions do I have for my Super Champions?

_____

_____

_____

_____

What am I requesting of each of them?

_____

_____

_____

_____

_____

What actions do I want them to take on my behalf?

_____

_____

_____

_____

Write Your Plan

Use the following pages to create your progress plan.

I AM HERE EMOTIONAL INTENTION ACTION TIMELINE

Gap

Progress Report

IMAGINE BEING IN A LIFE YOU LOVE

I AM HERE

INTENTION

ACTION

TIMELINE

HEALTH

Gap

Progress Report

I AM HERE

FINANCES

INTENTION

ACTION

TIMELINE

Gap

Progress Report

IMAGINE BEING IN A LIFE YOU LOVE

I AM HERE **INTENTION** **ACTION** **TIMELINE**

FAMILY

Gap

Progress Report

I AM HERE   INTENTION   ACTION   TIMELINE

FAITH

Gap

Progress Report

I AM HERE   INTENTION   ACTION   TIMELINE

FUN

Gap

Progress Report

I AM HERE   INTENTION   ACTION   TIMELINE

RELATIONSHIPS

Gap

Progress Report

I AM HERE INTENTION ACTION TIMELINE

CONTRIBUTION

Gap

Progress Report

TIMELINE

ACTION

INTENTION

I AM HERE

PERSONAL

Gap

Progress Report

I AM HERE   INTENTION   ACTION   TIMELINE

COMMUNITY

Gap

Progress Report

I AM HERE   INTENTION   ACTION   TIMELINE

EDUCATION

Gap

Progress Report

I AM HERE	INTENTION	ACTION	TIMELINE
VACATION			

Gap

Progress Report

I AM HERE   **INTENTION**   **ACTION**   **TIMELINE**

RELAXATION

Gap

Progress Report

I AM HERE INTENTION ACTION TIMELINE

WEALTH

Gap

Progress Report

I AM HERE   INTENTION   ACTION   TIMELINE

BUSINESS

Gap

Progress Report

I AM HERE   INTENTION   ACTION   TIMELINE

HOME

Gap

Progress Report

I AM HERE   INTENTION   ACTION   TIMELINE

OTHER

Gap

Progress Report

Play Your Choice Cards

What are the "ah buts" that could get in my way of achieving my intentions? What comes into my mind when I look at my plan for my life?

_____

_____

_____

Are my choices working for me? Are the choices helping me to progress toward a life I love? If so, how?

_____

_____

What do I choose to feel good about?

_____

_____

_____

What do I choose to feel badly about?

_____

_____

_____

How will I handle those things that I choose to feel badly about?

_____

_____

_____

_____

Who can help me deal with those things that I choose to feel badly about?

_____

_____

_____

_____

✦ PART THREE: IMAGINE BEING THE REASON

Remember, life does not always work out smoothly. It is full of PINGs, uncertainties, complexities, and change. You live in a vibrant, ever-changing world that requires you to be tolerant, flexible, adaptable, and agile. You have to bend and twist on the journey to deliver on your intentions. You may have to go round, over, or through obstacles to get to where you need to be. It may not simply work out in a straight line from A to Z.

Manage Life's PINGs

What have been the major PINGs in my life?

_____

_____

_____

_____

Are there some PINGs that have become reasons, explanations, or excuses for the way I live my life now, or that could adversely impact how my life will go in the future?

_____

_____

_____

_____

Which PINGs have unexpectedly made me stronger?

_____

_____

_____

_____

Here are the simple PINGs that affect my life:

_____

_____

_____

_____

Here are the significant PINGs that affect my life:

_____

_____

_____

_____

_____

Here are the swift PINGs that affect my life:

_____

_____

_____

_____

Here are the sweeping PINGs that affect my life:

_____

_____

_____

_____

_____

Where am I sensing a loss of power?

_____

_____

_____

_____

_____

What can I do about it, and who can I turn to?

_____

_____

_____

_____

_____

Develop Your Unshakable Belief System

Do I have a belief system in place to handle any obstacle I may come across? Describe it.

_____

_____

_____

_____

_____

Do I truly believe that realizing my intentions is possible? Why do I believe it?

_____

_____

_____

_____

_____

Why do I believe others will help me with my intentions?

_____

_____

_____

_____

_____

Why am I the constant in the midst of life's variables? What is it about me that will allow me to face all challenges?

_____

_____

_____

_____

_____

Master the Setbacks

Am I seeing my life as the creator or victim of it? Why?

_____

_____

_____

_____

What are the barriers I am seeing, and how can I overcome them?

_____

_____

_____

_____

Can I gain mastery over the setbacks? What will I need to improve in myself to gain this mastery?

_____

_____

_____

_____

If I cannot gain mastery over setbacks, what am I saying about them? What help do I need?

_____

_____

_____

_____

What help is currently available to me to get through the setbacks?

_____

_____

_____

_____

_____

If I am not getting what I want and the setbacks have stopped me, what new actions do I need to take now?

_____

_____

_____

_____

What do I notice about the reactions I have to setbacks?

_____

_____

_____

Do setbacks make me annoyed, frustrated, or angry? What alternative responses do I need to employ?

_____

_____

_____

Am I spending more than twenty-four hours complaining about what is happening to me? Have I outlived my Special Person Day (SPD)?

_____

_____

_____

_____

Where am I wallowing in my misfortunes? Am I willing to stop?

_____

_____

_____

_____

What is not going my way?

_____

_____

_____

What is getting in my way?

_____

_____

_____

How can I get through what is in my way?

_____

_____

_____

_____

How can I take back control of my life?

_____

_____

_____

_____

Make Course Corrections

What new actions can I now take to move forward with my imagined life?

_____

_____

_____

_____

Are there any course corrections I now need to make? What new paths or directions can I take?

_____

_____

_____

_____

Do I need to find a new purpose in my life?

_____

_____

_____

_____

Do I adapt easily to new actions or directions, or do I struggle to change?

_____

_____

_____

_____

What could I do to adapt more easily to change?

_____

_____

_____

_____

Do I need to review my plan for where I want to be in life? What changes do I see that I can make?

_____

_____

_____

_____

_____

What structure do I have in place to keep me on track with my intentions? If I do not have one, what do I need to do to keep on track?

_____

_____

_____

_____

_____

Is passive hostility crippling my dreams and leaving me powerless? If so, how can I replace the hostility with positive actions?

_____

_____

_____

_____

In order to identify what might be making me hostile, I need to first identify what is making me grateful for my life. Here is what I have now in my life:

_____

_____

_____

_____

Here is what I want in my life:

_____

_____

_____

_____

Here are those things I am being passively hostile about:

_____

_____

_____

_____

✦ PART FOUR: IMAGINE BEING THE ENERGY

Your energy is connected to your personal power, the power you have within yourself to take the necessary actions to be in a life that you love. Your personal power comes from being the cause of your life, creating and developing opportunities for what is important to you. Your energy comes from facing up to, taking hold of, and overcoming the setbacks that you experience. It is what will propel you forward to realizing your intentions and attaining your goals. Your energy will also attract others who bear witness to who you are and how you are showing up in the world, and their support will help you sustain. As you put one foot in front of the other, and take one action and then the next, you will find yourself in a new place of expectation.

Harness the Momentum

What gives me energy in my life? When, what, where, and with whom do I feel invigorated?

_____

_____

_____

_____

_____

Where do I experience a lack of energy? Do I need to avoid those things and people with whom I sense a lack of energy?

_____

_____

_____

_____

_____

What have I been focusing on as the priorities in my life?

_____

_____

_____

_____

What intentions have fallen by the wayside as I focused on the above? What will I do about it?

_____

_____

_____

_____

Where am I using displaced energy? Where am I caring too much for others and not caring enough for myself? How do I find a balance?

_____

_____

_____

_____

Where and with whom do I need to make new agreements about what time and attention I can give?

_____

_____

_____

_____

Are there any old agreements I have with my family, friends, colleagues, or others that I need to review now?

_____

_____

_____

_____

What new agreements do I need to put in place with them?

_____

_____

_____

_____

_____

Am I taking action—doing something each and every day—however small, to forward the momentum with my intentions? What could I be doing?

_____

_____

_____

_____

Who can help me remain on course with my intentions?

_____

_____

_____

_____

Where have I taken action? Where have I not taken action?

_____

_____

_____

_____

What do I need to do right now for actions I have not taken?

_____

_____

_____

_____

What is stopping me from taking these actions? What will I do about it? Whose help do I need?

_____

_____

_____

_____

Does each intention continue to be important to me? If so, what will I do? If not, what will I change?

_____

_____

_____

_____

_____

What are the costs and consequences of me not taking the actions necessary to forward my intentions?

_____

_____

_____

_____

If I look forward toward the end of my life and realize that I did not accomplish all that I set out to do, what will I say has stopped me?

_____

_____

_____

_____

_____

What will allow me to say, "Well done, you! You achieved your imagined life!"?

_____

_____

_____

_____

_____

_____

Use Your Personal Power

Am I following the Imagine Being method for being in a life I love?

I   – Instigate change and create a challenge for yourself.

M   – Move—take action!

A   – Access my inner confidence and belief system.

G   – Get over complaining.

I   – Involve my lifelines.

N   – Nurture my choices.

E   – Embrace and develop a plan.

B   – Be accountable.

E   – Eliminate my setbacks.

I   – Involve my Super Champions.

N   – Navigate my course corrections.

G   – Give and accept assistance.

Which of the above do I need to focus on more?

I _____

M _____

A _____

G _____

I _____

N _____

E _____

B _____

E _____

I _____

N _____

G _____

What questions do I have about the way forward for each of my intentions?

_____

_____

_____

_____

Whose help do I need in the areas noted above?

_____

_____

_____

_____

Share and Sustain Your Accomplishments

Do I believe in my own greatness? Why?

_____

_____

_____

What big accomplishments do I want to celebrate?

_____

_____

_____

_____

What small accomplishments do I want to celebrate?

_____

_____

_____

_____

How will I celebrate my accomplishments?

_____

_____

_____

How can I share my accomplishments with others?

_____

_____

_____

_____

Are there people I could coach, mentor, or advise on what I have accomplished for myself?

_____

_____

_____

_____

Are there any new or revised intentions I wish to make now (without becoming an intentions junkie!)?

_____

_____

_____

_____

Who do I need to support me in maintaining my accomplishments?

_____

_____

_____

_____

Have I used any of the following to help me set goals and celebrate my accomplishments?

Diary _____

Progress charts_____

Events _____

Storyboards and collages_____

Telephone calls and coaching_____

Committed listeners _____

✦ PART FIVE: IMAGINE BEING THE LIGHT

There exists a fifth element that will complete you. Being in a life you love means sharing love with those around you. It means being a light to others—your family, your friends, your co-workers, your church, your community, and your world. As you imagine being in a life you love and begin living it, you will realize that your light will shine from within. As the true you comes into being, others will notice your "magical presence." Your light will be a reflection of your spirit, your thoughts, your actions, and your beliefs.

Your Light

When I look at people who appear to have a magical presence, what do I notice about them?

_____

_____

_____

_____

Who has been the light for me?

_____

_____

_____

Where can I be the light for others?

_____

_____

_____

_____

From whom am I willing to accept help?

_____

_____

_____

_____

Who has offered me help in the past that I did not accept?

_____

_____

_____

_____

_____

_____

What ten ways can I bring light to others?

1. _____
2. _____
3. _____
4. _____
5. _____
6. _____
7. _____
8. _____
9. _____
10. _____

What ten places in my community can I bring light to others?

1. _____
2. _____
3. _____
4. _____
5. _____
6. _____
7. _____
8. _____
9. _____
10. _____

Who do I want to help immediately?

_____

_____

_____

_____

When I think about those people who have great meaning in my life, what did they do to earn that place in my heart?

_____

_____

_____

_____

How would I feel if someone acknowledged me as a light in their life?

_____

_____

_____

_____

Where, with whom, and in what way do I want to be the light for others?

_____

_____

_____

_____

_____

Who do I think would add me to their list of lifelines or Super Champions?

_____

_____

_____

_____

_____

Spreading the Light

Where do I believe people are in need and where do I want to help (without duty or obligation)?

_____

_____

_____

_____

_____

Who, specifically, needs my light right now?

_____

_____

_____

_____

_____

What do I see in the value of connecting?

_____

_____

_____

_____

_____

Who can I connect with in the coming weeks and months? How can I connect with them?

_____

_____

_____

_____

_____

What stories do I have to share that could help others with their lives?

_____

_____

_____

_____

How can I share my stories (e-mail, blogs, phone calls, meetings)?

_____

_____

_____

_____

Do I want to be a member of a global community devoted to reaching out to others, especially those in need?

_____

_____

_____

_____

Have I joined the *Imagine Being* Community (www.ImagineBeing.com)? If so, why? If not, why?

_____

_____

_____

_____

_____

✦ IMAGINE BEING

Imagine Being is, above all, about putting your dreams into action, making the impossible possible and the unreal real. You have the power within you to create the life you imagine for yourself. It starts with giving thought to what you believe will make you happier. You have the capacity to design a future for yourself—one that ignites the passion within you and excites you (and those around you). Now that you have completed the workbook, spend a few minutes writing where you imagine being twelve months from now.

_____

_____

_____

_____

_____

_____

_____

_____

_____

_____

_____

_____

_____

_____

_____

_____

_____

_____

_____

✦SUMMARY NOTES

Step into the intention of living your life *with* purpose and *on* purpose. Seize the very core of your being to participate in the present moment . . . every minute, every hour, every day. Focus on strengthening the core of your being by recognizing those areas within you that give you the power to realize your dreams.

- You, being the *cause* of designing your life
- You, being the *opportunity* maker in your life
- You, being the *reason* for momentum in your life
- You, being the *energy* responsible for your life
- You, being the *light* that guides the way for others

PART ONE: IMAGINE BEING THE CAUSE

In this section, you learned to:

- Take control of your life
- Recognize that what you cause has effect
- Take responsibility for your happiness and contentment
- Leave behind the TEMP excuses
- Define where you are and where you want to be
- Create a lifeline
- Hold yourself accountable

KEY POINTS:

Assess and Access the Life You Imagine

- Realize and accept that you alone *must* be responsible for your life.

- Become clear regarding exactly what you must be responsible for.

- Assess who you need to communicate with about your responsibility.

- Accept and forgive yourself for previous shortcomings.

- Ensure you learn so you don't repeat the same mistakes.

- Do not give in to the TEMP excuses (Time, Energy, Money, People).

Define Who and Where You Want to Be

- Gain control of your life by defining who you are and where you want to be.

- Assess your resistance to change by applying the Change Equation–D > (V + K + C) (D = dissatisfaction; V = vision; K = knowledge; C = costs, or consequences).

Create a Lifeline

- Identify and invite those people who you would like to help you with the intentions for your life.

- Request that your lifeline help you review what is important to you in life—family, career, faith, health, and whatever else is important and necessary for you to imagine being in the life you love.

- Talk to your lifeline about why your needs and wants are important to you.

- Write down the needs and wants and ask your lifeline for guidance in attaining them.

- Enlist your lifeline in helping you to overcome any obstacles.

Hold Yourself Accountable

- Box yourself in to box yourself out (put yourself in the position of having to accomplish your intentions by getting leverage on yourself).

- Send a monthly progress report to a lifeline.

- Declare your intentions publicly.

- Always keep your plan in front of you.
- Read, learn, and grow around the areas of your intentions, and discover the experts and model yourself after them.

PART TWO: IMAGINE BEING THE OPPORTUNITY

In this section you learned to:
- Take advantage of the Big O
- Be the author of your life
- Reject the "ah buts"
- Declare your intentions
- Identify your Super Champions
- Play your choice cards
- Write your plan

KEY POINTS:

Take Advantage of the Big O
- Take advantage of the opportunities in life and overcome the setbacks and excuses that can hold you back.
- Remember that Circumstances + Action = Opportunity.

Be the Author of Your Possibilities
- LIP Service–Change the original definition of lip service from talk only to expanding the associated possibilities and acting on them—Living In Possibility.

Declare Your Intentions
- Place focused attention on assessing your intentions.
- Write your intention, including an exact measurement, time frame, and result.
- Identify your Super Champions (those people you do not personally know who can support you with specific intentions).

Write Your Plan
- Write a clear plan for your life by declaring your intentions and identifying the choices you have.
- Identify areas of focus and list your intentions.
- Identify your gaps (what is between you and your goals).

- Define your actions (what steps are necessary for you to take).
- Obtain leverage on yourself (state why your intentions are important).
- Assess your progress and make adjustments where needed.
- Contact your Super Champions.

Play Your Choice Cards

- Acknowledge that you have infinite choices available to you, as well as their results and consequences.
- Reject the "ah buts"—the reasons, excuses, or explanations that will keep you from your goals.
- Choose well and wisely when making decisions in life.

PART THREE: IMAGINE BEING THE REASON

In this section you learned to:

- Address the PINGs in life
- Develop your unshakable belief system
- Master the setbacks
- Take SPDs
- Make course corrections

KEY POINTS:

Life PINGs

- Realize that "stuff" will happen in life and that you must adapt, move on, and utilize what you learn to empower yourself and others.
- The Crests (good PINGs) are those things that can impact your life for the better.
- The Troughs (bad PINGs) come in four types: Simple, Significant, Swift, and Sweeping.
- To gain power over the PINGs, the must remain in power, in control of your life.

Develop Your Unshakable Belief System

- Accept that you will have challenges in life and develop a belief system that will sustain your dreams and hold you accountable to them.

- Remember the XY Equation when outside forces impact your desired goals (where X is the variable, and Y is you, the constant).

Master the Setbacks

- Gain mastery over the problems, difficulties, and issues in life.

- Be willing to make it happen for yourself no matter what—change, take another approach, create new opportunities, and talk to people to help you through any situation.

- Take an SPD (Special Person Day) when the PINGs get you down.

Make Course Corrections

- Don't be afraid to take a new path to or new direction if your original plans are not working.

- Passive Hostility–Recognize the behavior that arises when you want something you are not getting.

PART FOUR: IMAGINE BEING THE ENERGY

In this section you learned to:

- Harness momentum

- Use your personal power

- Share and sustain your accomplishments

KEY POINTS:

Harness the Momentum

- Remember that most change happens one small step or choice by one small step or choice.

- Stay tuned in to your entire life, your whole plan with all of its intentions, and give each your focus and energy.

- Keep in action every day of your life.

Use Your Personal Power

- Realize first and foremost that you have the power within you to cause change.

- Commit yourself to conscious consideration and conscious action.

- Remember the IMAGINE BEING acronym:

    I—Instigate change and create a challenge for yourself.

    M—Move—take action!

    A—Access your inner confidence and belief system.

    G—Get over complaining.

    I—Involve your lifelines.

    N—Nurture your choices.

    E—Embrace and develop a plan.

    B—Be accountable.

    E—Eliminate your setbacks.

    I—Involve your Super Champions.

    N—Navigate your course corrections.

    G—Give and accept assistance.

Sustain and Share Your Accomplishments

- Realize that there is greatness in you.
- Share your results with others, both the successes and the setbacks.
- Sustain your accomplishments by creating a structure to keep to them.

PART FIVE: IMAGINE BEING THE LIGHT

In this section you learned about:

- Spread the light
- Assess your light
- Continue the light

KEY POINTS:

Your Light

- Identify how you can be a light in the lives of others.
- Identify opportunities (places) where you can shine your light on others.

Spread the Light

- Imagine yourself in the shoes of someone who is suffering or in pain.

- Make a connection—reach out to someone who you know could use a helping hand or a friendly smile.
- Make a difference by joining the *Imagine Being* Community.

Continue the Light

- Share your stories and those of others you know who have been the light in someone else's life.

RESOURCES

Books

- *Man's Search for Meaning* by Viktor Frankl
- *Living, Loving & Learning* by Leo Buscaglia and Steven Short
- *You Can Make It Happen: A Nine Step Plan for Success* by Stedman Graham
- *The Seven Spiritual Laws of Success: A Practical Guide to the Fulfillment of Your Dreams* by Deepak Chopra
- *Chicken Soup for the Soul* (Series) by Mark Victor Hansen and Jack Canfield
- *The Ten Commitments: Translating Good Intentions to Great Choices* by David Simon and Deepak Chopra
- *The Purpose Driven Life: What On Earth Am I Here For* by Rick Warren
- *The Dark Side of the Light Chasers: Reclaiming Your Power, Creativity, Brilliance and Dreams* by Debbie Ford
- *Your Best Life Now: 7 Steps to Living at Your Full Potential* by Joel Osteen
- *The Last Word on Power: Executive Re-Invention for Leaders Who Must Make The Impossible Happen* by Tracy Goss

- *The Three Laws of Performance: Rewriting the Future of Your Organization and Your Life* (J.B. Warren Bennis Series) by Steve Zaffron and Dave Logan

- *The Way of the Wizard: 20 Lessons for Living a Magical Life* by Deepak Chopra

- *Synchrodestiny: Harnessing the Infinite Power of Coincidence to Create Miracles* by Deepak Chopra

- *Unlimited Power: The New Science of Personal Achievement* by Anthony Robbins

- *Awaken the Giant Within: How to Take Immediate Control of Your Mental, Emotional, Physical and Financial Destiny!* by Anthony Robbins

Organizations

The Chopra Center (www.chopra.com)

Landmark Education (www.landmarkeducation.com)

S. Graham & Associates (www.stedmangraham.com)

VSA Consulting (www.vsacoach.com)

ONE Campaign (www.one.org)

Anthony Robbins Companies (www.tonyrobbins.com)

SUCCESS Magazine (www.success.com)

✦ABOUT THE AUTHORS

KRISTIN ANDRESS

Kristin Andress is the CEO of Andress Consulting, based in Solana Beach, California. Andress Consulting has been in business since 2002 and brings to clients the value proposition of exploring their ideas, passions, or visions—and exploding them to the possibilities. Kristin consults with authors, businesses, and entrepreneurs to create business, marketing, and promotional strategies; and craft key messages and the collateral to describe and position the person, product, or service offerings. She specializes in getting into the fabric of her clients' lives, work, or businesses, and simplifies what is seemingly complex. In doing so, her clients become laser-focused and clear, which leads to creating the connections with complementary businesses, media, and distribution avenues required to generate scale.

Prior to launching Andress Consulting, Kristin enjoyed a ten-year career with Arthur Andersen, serving as Director of Tax and Legal–Performance and Learning. She led global operations of a fifty-two person team in the United States and had coordination oversight with teams in Cambridge, England, and Asia-Pacific, with responsibility for a multi-million dollar budget.

Kristin holds a bachelor's degree in Public Communication/Human Relations from Western Illinois University and a master's degree in Organizational Communication from the University of Missouri-Columbia.

Kristin enjoyed growing up in the small town of Pittsfield, Illinois, and regularly returns to visit family. Short stays are coupled with the niggling need to rub in her return to the ocean air and golf courses of Solana Beach, California, where she resides. Kristin can be reached at kristin@ImagineBeing.com

JAQUI JEANES-LOWRY

Jaqui Jeanes-Lowry is an executive coach and consultant to some of the world's major public limited companies (PLCs) and private companies. As the managing partner of VSA Consulting Inc., United Kingdom and EMEA, she works with executives and professionals in the manufacturing, engineering, retail, aerospace, pharmaceutical, agrochemical, technology, and financial industries as well as the public health sector.

Jaqui coaches to cause transformation in individuals and businesses. She uses unique methodologies to change mindsets that change behaviours, allowing individuals to break through in their thinking to transform their business and lives. Jaqui is known for generating unprecedented, unpredictable results in short amounts of time.

Previously, Jaqui owned her own training and coaching company, delivering leadership and coaching programmes to more than 300 senior managers and executives. Prior to that, she was a HRD specialist for two major retail PLCs, and an operational manager in a major retail PLC where she became fully conversant in business and leadership.

Jaqui was also a director for Transformation Africa Ltd, an NFP company that developed a programme for personal development and leadership in South Africa. Her vision was to create a global leadership programme, delivered by personal development experts, that would give people practical advice and guidance on how to make a difference for themselves and their communities. This initiative led to a conference at the Johannesburg headquarters of Vodacom with stakeholders in South Africa on establishing what the issues were and what was needed to move things forward. The participants included individuals who ran large empowerment programmes, community leaders, academics, corporate change leaders, media members and journalists, and not-for-profit leaders. It also led to a community workshop in Nelspruit, Mpumalanga, where many local people came forward to look at how they could change themselves and their community.

Jaqui travels extensively to listen to and experience current thinking in business, leadership, and personal development. She also surrounds herself with a dream team of personal coaches and mentors, and thrives on expanding her network of executives, friends, visionaries, and general corporate contacts, always listening for how she may be of assistance and how she can connect people.

Jaqui was born in the United Kingdom and graduated from the University of Huddersfield with a BSc in Behavioural Sciences. She is a licensed practitioner of Neuro-Linguistic Programming (NLP) and a member of the European Mentoring Centre. She currently spends her time between Yorkshire and London in England, and Mallorca, Spain. She can be reached at jaqui@ImagineBeing.com.